A **HISTORY** OF
HUNGARIAN MUSIC

D1799615

A **HISTORY** OF **HUNGARIAN MUSIC**

László Dobszay

Corvina

Based on a revised version of the following
Hungarian edition: *Magyar Zenetörténet*, Budapest, 1984
English translation by Mária Steiner
Translation revised by Paul Merrick
Design by Simon Koppány

On the cover:
Concert of the Angels (14. c.)
(painted wooden sculpture)
Christian Museum, Esztergom

This volume has been published with support from the
Magyar Könyv Alapítvány (Hungarian Book Foundation).

ISBN 963 13 3498 8

Printed in Hungary, 1993
Photolettering Print-Tech Ltd. Budapest
Dürer Printing House, Gyula

Contents

1 The Beginnings of Hungarian Music

In 926, a mounted group of armed men approached the south German monastery of St Gall. Frightened by news of the latest marauding expeditions of the pagan Magyars, the monks fled, leaving behind only Heribald, a simple-minded friar. The Hungarian raiders made Heribald open up the cloister's cellars and, while carousing and revelling, called to their gods. Later they made Heribald and the cleric they had brought with them as interpreter sing their own songs, as it were by way of a response. When the two began to chant the Gregorian antiphon for the Feast of the Holy Cross, which was due the following day, the Magyars surrounded them and listened in amazement to this chant, unusual to their ears. But a bugle-call came from the sentries, warning the revellers of the approach of an enemy, so they drew up in battle array and hurriedly left.

What were those shouts to their gods like? What sounds came out of the "speaking" bugle? These questions were left unanswered by Eckehardt, the chronicler of the "St Gall adventure".

By the time of this St Gall episode, the Hungarians, who with the last wave of migration had reached the borders of Latin Europe, had been terrorizing the West for thirty years with their marauding raids, and were to do so for another twenty years or so. These raids, combining politics and strategy with plunder, took the Magyars as far as Italy and Spain, from Byzantium to the Atlantic. *A sagittis Hungarorum libera nos Domine* (From the arrows of the Hungarians, deliver us, Lord) was chanted in the invocations of litanies throughout Europe.

Where did this confederation of tribes come from who found a homeland for themselves within Europe–first physically, in the thinly populated region of what was than Pannonia, long without political power, and then after a few decades, spiritually also? Is anything known of their ancient music in those centuries from which scarcely any written records survive?

Linguistically they belonged to the Finno-Ugrian family of peoples. Until the fifth or sixth century AD the tribes forming the core of what later became the Magyar people lived a life of fishing and hunting somewhere in the region of the Volga and Káma rivers, west of the Ural Mountains. They then set out southwards, towards the northern coast of the Black Sea, where they joined the ethnic community of the Turkic empires which followed one another in the region (ending under Khazar supremacy). During the following four or five centuries, the Magyars learned agriculture and animal husbandry, and the formidable tactic of fighting and shooting arrows on horseback. They also became acquainted with a more highly organized, centralized statecraft, and besides the Turks, were influenced by the material and intellectual culture of the Iranians, the Byzantines and the Slavs. Their ethnic composition also underwent a change. By the late ninth century, when, yielding to the pressure of peoples arriving from the Orient they moved first to the *Etelköz* (the outer border of the Carpathians), and then entered the Carpathian Basin (*c.* 896), their members included a considerable number of Khazars, Turks and other peoples.

Historical data exists which seems to initiate the existence of certain musical forms at the time. The important genres we may surmise to have been practiced, learnt or assimilated by the ancient Magyar tribes were ritual epic songs, incantations, possibly accompanied on primitive instruments, "shaman chants", heroic lays and lyrical songs of the warlike eastern peoples, and the vocal folk customs of the ancient European cultures living close to nature, transmitted by the Slavs and Byzantines (e.g. the rituals of the winter and summer solstices).

The Earliest Folk-song Types

For a more substantial knowledge of the music itself one has to turn to folk music. Comparative musicology can distinguish with a fair degree of certainty those styles in twentieth century folk music which are in fact the remains of traditions dating from the settlement of the Hungarians in their present-day homeland. Of course this is not a matter of survival without change, but rather the preservation of significant elements of style.

These elements include a few primitive, rhythmic songs of two or three notes that have come down to us in certain children's songs and folk customs. Originally these may have been associated with nature magic (which their words often refer to) as well.*

CMPH I. No. 45

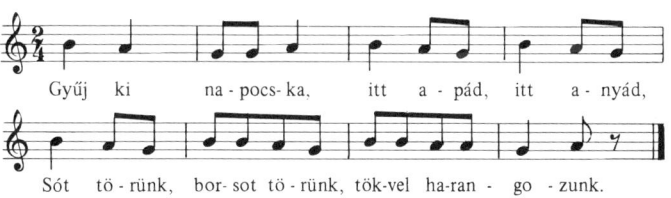

(Come out, little sun, here's your mother, here's your father, we crush salt, we crush pepper, we chime with a pumpkin.)

---

* Examples of folk-music are given in simple notation, pieces from the sixteenth and seventeenth centuries in diminished rhythmic values, and larger works in short score.

Other styles include two types of recitative, one diatonic and the other pentatonic. Originally these may have consisted of improvised melodies using traditional formulae, joined to words of a ritual nature, relating the memory of ancestors. Twentieth century improvised folk laments seem to closely approximate to this original state. Musically, both styles are unrestricted as to form and number of syllables, and both use range of 3 to 4 notes which are rarely expanded upwards, but nearly always downwards, at the end of single strophes:

a)   Extract from a lament. CMPH V, No. 205.

Ó drá-ga egy jó pá-rom né-kem,   de itt hagytál in - ge-met,

ár- ván is a gyermeke-id- del,   ár- ván is a te gyer-me-keid-del . . .(etc.)

(Oh my dear, my only good mate, how you left mere here forsaken,
with your children, forsaken with your children.)

b)   Extract from a lament. CMPH V, No. 199

...Hogy tud-jam el- fe - lej - te- ni   é - des-a - nyám,

hogy én nem tudtam ken - det el - ké - sér - ni ma - mám.

Hogy tud-nám bár ál-momba meg- lát - ni,   má - mi-kám, mámi-kám,

hogy ké-sér-ték el   a töb-bi test-vé-re - im, ma-mám, é- des-a - nyám,   jaj!

(How can I forget, mother, that I could not accompany you, mum?
How could I see at least in my dream, dear little mummy mine,
dear little mummy mine,
how my brothers and sisters accompanied you, mum, mother mine, oh!?)

The two styles are also similar in that later on (whether before the Hungarian conquest or during the Middle Ages has not been established), this recitative raw material gave rise to strophic melodies, naturally with new texts (laments, ballads, lyrical songs, etc.).

Both styles have counterparts among the Finno-Ugrian (and in part the Old Turcic) peoples with whom the ancient Magyars lived in the Volga region. And both also have Gregorian equivalents, which indicates a wide distribution, mainly in Mediterranean. Thus they are probably particular versions of a wider European recitative style, reshaped as a result of contact with different languages and tastes. Whether some geographic, ethnic or functional division lies behind the two tonally different but otherwise related styles can only be a matter of conjecture. As it happens, the pentatonic recitative style and its strophic derivatives are today only found among the Hungarians of Transylvania.

Descending Pentatonic Melodies

Modern folk-music research began early in the twentieth century, the pentatonic descending fifth-shift melody was considered to be the most ancient style because of its char-

acteristic eastern counterparts and its divergences from its
European environment.

CMPH VI, No. 414.

Rö - püjj pá - va, rö - püjj,   Vár - mö-gye há - zá - ra,
A   sze-gény ra - bok-nak   Sza - ba - du -lá - sá - ra.

*(Fly, peacock, fly, to the county hall,
to free the poor captives.)*

This undoubtedly represents a tradition reaching back to
before the Hungarian conquest, a rich stock of melodies
which has served over a long period to determine the fla-
vour of Hungarian music, in the case of the peasantry practically up to the present day. It is also true that its distance
from European music of the period from the fifteenth to
the nineteenth centuries as well as its high aesthetic value
justify the attraction it exercised on twentieth-century
composers desirous of evolving a modern art music that
broke with an impoverished major–minor tonality.

Nevertheless, today this pentatonic style is held to be
later than the recitative-rooted music just discussed, probably dating from the time when the Magyar tribes lived
in the Black Sea region. In contrast to the pentatonic and
diatonic recitative styles, it is a basically melody-oriented
style, marked by broadly arched melodic lines, expressive
interval steps, with often a free (rubato) manner of performance, rich ornamentation and lyrical words. Recording
of similar pentatonic music have been made among Turkic
and Tatar peoples, where, however, one finds lengthier,
more profuse and unregulated flow of melody. The melody
begins at a high emotional temperature and in a high reg-

ister, descending and sweeping back in waves repeatedly, without the articulation of deliberate motivic repetitions. Hungarian melodies on the other hand, are typified by different regularities of lines equal length (isosyllabic), a four-line structure, a characteristic arrangement of line-ending notes (cadences), a graduated descent together with motivic correspondences, in many cases leading to the second half of the melody being a repetition of the first a fifth lower (the so-called "fifth-shift").

How did this style develop? Melodic adjustment probably began under the mutual influence of two factors. The shorter lines, approximately or exactly of equal length, may have led to the stabilization of musical rhymes and correspondences. They also assisted the dominance of the line-ending (cadence) notes, the fifth in the middle of the melody, and the keynote at the end (at first only serving to make the total order clear) prompting the singer to adapt the melody at these points, and bring them into a fifth-oriented relationship.

Some of the melodies do not go beyond suggesting a fifth correspondance at the more important points. These melodies have the richest melodic content.

CMPH VI, No. 389.

Bá - nat,   bá - nat,   csuk - ros   bá - nat,

Mé rak - tál szí - vem - re vá - rat?

(Grief, grief, a cluster of grief,
why have you built a castle upon my heart?)

Others–particularly dance tunes in a strict rhythm–carry through the fifth correspondence over a longer section, or even the whole melody.

The point of departure was the so-called "Turkic" descending pentatonic melody (it is not clear whether this was associated with an ethnic or a geographical factor). According to present knowledge, its organization into a "fifth shifting" style took place among the Magyar people perhaps sometime between the sixth and ninth centuries.

Old Custom-tunes

The ancient Hungarian tribes came into contact with Slavs and Byzantines, as well as the Turkic peoples, also being affected by their culture. As these contacts continued after the conquest, becoming even stronger, it is more difficult to determine exactly when these later styles were incorporated. The folk customs and custom-tunes regulated by the calendar of the natural year, are mainly related to the traditions of the neighbouring Slav and Balkan peoples, through them having contact with the traditions of ancient pagan Europe, and occasionally also of Antiquity. These customs include, for instance, the sung fertility rite on St Lucy's day (13 December) and other cults linked with the winter solstice, the Sundays of welcoming the spring, and the summer solstice (Midsummer Night, 24 June). Some of these were enriched in the Middle Ages by new poetic and musical elements deriving from the church, school and court life, so it is not easy to separate the different historical layers. The tunes relating to Midsummer Night, at least, are definitely rooted in the culture of late Antiquity or the early Middle Ages.

CMPH II, No. 232

Tü - zit meg-ra - kat - ta, vi -lá - gos Szent Já - nos,

Fe - hír - ha -jú Ma - gyar I - lo - na,

Ha - ján fö - lű gyöngyko - szo-rú gyöngy... (etc.)

(St John, the bringer of light, had his fire laid. Refrain: White-haired Ilona Magyar, a wreath of pearls, of pearls upon her hair.)

Of course it is never a matter of simple borrowing. A new element is blended with elements of the old tradition, becoming reinterpreted under their influence and forming a new unit with them.

An example is the custom of *regölés** on the evening of 25 December, which remains a living tradition in southern Transdanubia and Transylvania, two border regions of the Hungarian speaking territory. Young lads walk through the village chanting a fertility magic incantation. According to linguists, the words which are repeated as a refrain in these loosely strung together songs of twin-bar motifs ("hej regö rejtem") are a term taken from ancient Finno-Ugrian shamanistic magic (joining words calling the gods and indicating entrancement). The unusual melody of the refrain however, returns to the fifth of the pentachord (which feels unfinished to a modern sense of tonality) such a type of refrain being found also in the corpus of Balkan folk music. As an ancient Byzantine ritual invocation, it shares its origin with the melody of the famous cry "Hagios ho Theos" on Good Friday.

CMPH II. No. 865

(*There is snowing–hey, ho, reme, róma,
rabbits, foxes are gambolling, hey, ho, reme, róma.*)

The freer, hymnic performance of the Byzantine invocation however is transformed in the *regös* song following the old manner of magic incantation using motivic repetition, the melodic line being fashioned accordingly.

This is not the end of its story. Later the complete forms of *regölés* became enriched with Christian motifs, elements of legends and mystery play images, and approached the form of the early medieval rondeau. The singers of this new form introduced themselves as the servants of St Stephen, as did the singers of the Western European festival greetings who were called *Stephansknechte*, i.e. servants of the Christian protomartyr, on the eve of whose feast they sang their *regölés*. The Hungarian singer, however, was also the servant of another St Stephen, the first Hungarian king (King Stephen the Saint, ruled 1000–1038). By announcing this, he was also stating that the *regös* now carried on this ancient custom under the protection of the saint King, released from the accusation of being pagan, and integrated into the new, Christian way of life.

2 The Early Middle Ages

(11th–13th Centuries)

In 1028, about a hundred years after the "St Gall episode", Arnoldus, a monk from Regensburg, arrived in Esztergom, the seat of the Hungarian kings and the Hungarian primate. A highly cultivated scholar of European renown, Arnoldus was in correspondence with the leading intellectual centres of the Latin world. Now he wanted to find out what the Archbishop of Esztergom thought of the new office he had written in honour of St Emmeran, patron saint of the monastery of Regensburg to replace the old clumsy words and music, but which, however, had met with opposition at home. The new office was studied in Esztergom, where it found favour. The following day, the feast of the saint, the cathedral choir included the new words and melody when they sang the liturgy.

What road had led to the descendants of the marauders now welcoming the monk as a brother? To a people not long previously calling to their gods now singing the liturgical chant which earlier they had listened to in awe?

If the *regös* singers discussed in the previous chapter called themselves the servants of King Stephen, the Hungarian nation as a whole can be said with even greater justification to have been the disciples of the king. As a versified office from the thirteenth century put it, Stephen turned the Hungarians' *crudelitas* into *credulitas*, and the poet, searching for an image to express the change, chose the voice which yesterday was roaring menacingly, and now sings sweet, well articulated songs:

Magnus Samson ad domandum leonem immittitur / ad Hungaros praedicandum rex fortis eligitur, / ex leonis fauce mellis favus gratus nascitur, / ex Hungari ore dulcis Deo laus exprimitur.

It calls for the great Samson to vanquish the lion, a strong king is sent to preach for the Hungarians, from the lion's throat there dribbles sweet honey, from the lips of the Hungarians there flows the sweet praise of God.

Evangelization began in the 970s, during the reign of Prince Géza (972–997), King Stephen's father. Géza had divided loyalties, feeling powerful enough to sacrifice to both the old good and the new simultaneously. His conversion, therefore and possibly that of many others, was fairly ambivalent, and only undergone as a kind of tactical manoeuvre. His son, Stephen (ruled as prince from 997, crowned king in 1000, died in 1038), however, turned to Christianity wholeheartedly and undertook the historical mission of integrating the Hungarians within Europe. A welding together of contrasting requirements strength and graciousness, cultivation and hard fighting, religious feeling and masterful domestic and foreign policies, opening gates wide to Europe and a firm defence of the country's independence formed the secret of his speedy achievements.

Vir beatum pardum nempe fert ad caulas ovium, / et leonem ad praesepe bovis ferocissimum, / nam minis, precibus et donis terret, mulcet, incitat, / pravos, mites, vanos, bonis Christi quos deificat.

(The holy man carries the panther into the sheepfold, / having the ferocious lion placed at the manger, / he asks and gives, threatens and calls, chases, urges / both the evil and the meek, who he sanctifies in Christ.)

But Stephen was not just a king, he was a *doctor et apostolus* as well, possessing great religious learning and the right to ecclesiastical organization. He founded ten episcopates, and to hinder foreign domination, raised Esztergom to an archbishopric over the Hungarian church.

Political and religious changes went hand in hand with the introduction of European culture and education. Records from the years of Stephen's reign speak of schools in Esztergom, Fehérvár, and Csanád, and the acquisition of the necessary teachers and books. At first schools were founded only in episcopal sees, but they were soon followed by schools in deaneries and on county bailiffs' estates later by municipal ones and schools run by the new churches ordered to be built one to every ten villages.

This educational system also provided a home for musical culture. Work in schools centred round the two principal subjects of grammar and music. A teacher of music from King Stephen's time is known by name: a certain master Walter. Listening to the song of a maid-servant as she turned the stone handmill, he was asked by his bishop: "what kind of carmen or secular song is this?" Walter's reply called it the *Symphonia Hungarorum.*

School instruction of singing was closely linked to the work of choirs in church, and so was much closer to everyday life than the musical education of later centuries. Students as a body daily joined the liturgy sung by the priests during the mass and main offices. Although the amount of sung material differed depending on the size of the school and the choir, its essence was the same in town and village alike: Gregorian chant, the highest art music of the period which regulated with unquestioned authority the musical activity of choirs and schools.

Through Gregorian chant Hungarian singers and schools were incorporated into a common European concert. Its requirements were a knowledge of Latin, of a form of articulated singing, precise in key and form, and of a repertoire of some 2,000-3,000 chants (at first from memory, and from the twelfth century onwards, with the help of notation), as well as of basic musical theory (intervals, solmization, musical notation, keys and modes). This shared European art still left room, however, for local characteristics to appear.

Choirs and Schools

When speaking of Hungarian specialities, it should be stressed that practically all of them can be traced back to foundations from St Stephen's time, all of them being adhered to by tradition over many centuries, slowly developing their inherent possibilities. We will begin with some observations on musical life, then continue with the music itself.

The cathedral and parish churches remained decisive factors in musical culture for two or three centuries, in fact throughout the Middle Ages. All the pupils in these schools received essentially the same, intensive plainsong education. Educated laymen shared the experience of sung liturgy for two or three hours a day, sharing a knowledge of musical notation, technique and theory, namely everything, in the eyes of their contemporaries, elevated music from the level of *usus* (mere practice) to the height of *ars* (artistry). Although there are records of more able children being selected for a soloistic part, or later to sing polyphonic pieces (as later it became general practice in the late Middle Ages to have two to four children to lead the singing of the whole choir, ["chorare"] i.e. the dignitaries, priests, chaplains and pupils, during more simple masses and offices) in Hungary, in contrast to Western Europe, it never happened that a choir of selected boys replaced the corpus of all the pupils. This might be the explanation for the somewhat conservative yet at the same time "democratic" character of late medieval Hungarian liturgical singing. The two are related, the explanation for them lying in the existence of a nation-wide, stable educational system. This is borne out by the vast number of notations in cursive handwriting found in late medieval musical manuscripts (stemming from literate people and not professional musicians or copyists), and by data, for instance, concerning groups of students welcoming noblemen in Gregorian chant, or laymen singing Latin chants, if necessary at sight.

Another characteristic of liturgical singing in Hungary is that its chief strength rested upon the network of episcopal sees and parishes. Although a great many Benedictine monks came from Italy, Germany and Bohemia to take part in the work of conversion, the foundation of Christianity in Hungary took place not as a long, fairly spontaneous process but instead within the framework of the ecclesiastical organization established by King Stephen. The work of the monks therefore also became integrated into the life of the "secular" churches, thus becoming the property of the whole nation. Both in the early days and later too, the monasteries were other eminent workshops of intellectual and religious life, living their daily round, singing the chant and enriching Hungarian culture with their work, writings and translations. In the thirteenth century, for example, some of the religious orders did very much for the development of Hungarian theology and learning, and others, in the fourteenth and fifteenth centuries, for the development in vernacular. But the medieval liturgical singing culture and musical notation which provided the basis for all this became a public affair, and evolved a tradition through the network of chapter and parish schools. Anything typically Hungarian in this field was almost always connected with the secular churches, the monasteries only lending colour to the general picture through their own musical material which was mostly of foreign origin. Nor did the confraternities, guilds, professional musicians and baronial residences play a major part in shaping and maintaining liturgical vocal culture. They appeared on the scene only in the second half of the Middle Ages, to introduce and perpetuate various polyphonic forms and other variegated musical material.

The third Hungarian characteristic springs from the proportion of and inter-relationship between unity and enriching differences. In Hungary one cannot speak of a multi-centred (liturgical) culture as existed for instance in Germany, Poland or Italy. At the same time, major local difference (the Esztergom and Kalocsa provinces), and within them special local traditions, surface within this essential unity. Waves of local initiative either regained the centre or retained their local colour within the whole. Only in the second half of the Middle Ages do we encounter separate traditions, breaking away from the whole or supplementing it, in the liturgical music of certain regions, towns or institutions. These classifiable differences and the basic unity is also related to the conditions of their foundation of Christianity here: the church organization, brought about purposefully by a strong central power, starting from scratch, and extending over a large sectionized territory.

Plainsong Varieties

But where does unity and difference emerge if this liturgical music is nothing more than the mere borrowing of a standardized European musical repertory?

A study of the repertoire makes it clear that part of the plainsong material (in the case of the mass a larger proportion, in that of the office a smaller one) is common to Europe actually the derivative of a tradition in late Antiquity. Its singers are at home anywhere in Europe.

Yet since it is not a matter of the discretionary succession of single chants, but rather an organic, cyclic whole, then the effectiveness of individual chants is determined by the very system of the liturgy. The Esztergom liturgy, which served as a model for local liturgies, evolved by the second half of the twelfth century at the latest, some at least of its elements certainly reaching back to the eleventh century. In its balance between well arranged orderliness and richness, the Hungarian liturgy had its own qualities, and adhered conscious to its traditions until the seventeenth century (1630).

The European layer of the Gregorian chant had variants in Hungary as well. Since in plainsong a single dimension of music–melody–prevails (as one cannot speak either of polyphony or of rhythm in a strict sense), then the various varieties have a much greater influence on the inner dimensions of the melody, its shape and content than in later styles. These variants are not capricious either, they are related to each other, and produce a kind of characteristic sound. Certain notes may stand out as focal points or as melodic backbone, changing the character of the tonality, and the balance of the melody.

Around 1000 AD, the European plainsong tradition became divided into two major units: the same melodies were either sung in a more elaborate manner, filling each interval with tiny scales, or in a style which stressed the pentatonic backbone of the melodic sections, showing a propensity for larger intervals. Of course there were many grades between the two. The first was mainly typical of Italy, France and England, and certain monastic orders. The other figured within a belt running from the Netherlands to Poland, including Northern Italy and part of Scandinavia as well. Hungary belonged to this latter, "pentatonicizing" dialect. But even the territory of the dialect was not uniform within itself. The group of Hungarian melodic variants can clearly be separated within it, with a highly uniform "central" tradition and local or peripheral practices joined to it. It would be difficult to give a general description of this "Hungarian" variant, as it can only be apprehended in the concrete arrangement of the various chants and the choice of their inner proportions, turning points and basic notes. All we can say in words perhaps is that a large-scale fashioning, aimed at stressing essential motifs is more strongly perceptible in it than in those of the neighbouring countries.

Liber Usualis; the Passau Printed Gradual,
see Das Erbe deutscher Musik, Vol. 87, Kassel etc., 1982, f 20;
Missale Notatum Strigoniense, f 22 (Musicalia Danubiana 1.)

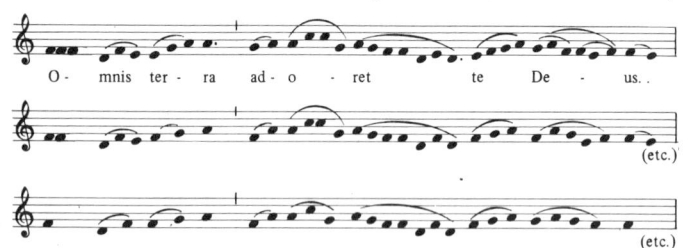

(May all the lands worship You, God...)

Regional Melodies

Besides the chants common to Europe, the repertoire of liturgical plainsong also included "regional" melodies. These emerge in certain regions or at certain isolated points, and their origin can rarely be established with certainty. They might be ancient chants that became extinct, only surviving in a few traditions or regions. Thus, for instance, there are scarcely any records in Europe of one particular Holy Week respond of eastern origin ("Vadis propitiator") which belonged to the fundamental layer of the liturgy in Hungary. In other cases, a local composition achieved great popularity in its own environment and became incorporated into the standard customs of a wide range of liturgical centres. Such, for instance, is the cycle of antiphons "A diebus antiquis" of unknown origin, which opens the Advent season, and which features in a Hungarian source as early as the twelfth century, also forming a standard element of later Hungarian chant as well. It can also be found in late medieval sources from Salzburg, Passau and Cracow. In other cases a regional piece or cycle gained popularity, but only *ad libitum*, known to one community or in one source, and unknown in others. The Office of St Gall, for instance, came to Hungary from Southern Germany, but was not welcomed everywhere. In Regensburg manuscripts there is an interesting trope which introduced the "return" of the Alleluia for Easter eve ("Jam domnus optatas"). This remained a constant element of the liturgy in Hungary up till the seventeenth century.

Regional chants in many cases became vehicles for new styles. For in liturgical singing built on plainsong we encounter ever new musical layers that enriched and developed the auditory realm of the singer of the day (new developments in the ninth, eleventh and thirteenth centuries). Regarding local repertoires, here all bodies of tradition are more discriminating in their selections. Also typical of Hungarian Gregorian chant is what it borrowed and how firmly and where it incorporated borrowings into its own customs.

For instance, the place a chant is to occupy within its new environment is not immaterial either. A chant addressed to the Virgin Mary, which recalls the style of the turn of the millennium ("Ave spes nostra") and occurs sporadically in European sources, occupies a fixed place in the Prague rite, where it is sung at the procession which concludes the vespers for Advent. It also became a significant part of the Hungarian liturgy, but in a different form. Before the vespers for 24 December began the Christmas

celebrations, the first Ave ("Ave spes nostra") was sung
by two children in a dark corner of the church, in surplices,
with lighted candles in their hands. They then started towards the choir before the altar, being joined by another
couple coming from an other corner of the church, singing
"Ave, illud ave...". A third pair set off from the middle of
the church, singing "Ave concipiens...", and by the time
they all reached the choir, the whole congregation was
singing: "Ave, casta..."

Antiphonale Strigoniense secundum usum ordinis Paulinorum,
Zagreb, Bibl. Univ. MR 8. p. 39.

*(Hail, our hope, chaste mother of God. Hail, you, who received
that Ave Maria from the angel. Hail, you, who conceived the
Father's brightness, you blessed one. Hail, chaste, holy virgin...)*

Hungarian Composed Chants

The third layer, beside the general and the regional chants,
consists of local–in this case–Hungarian compositions.
Naturally these are the hardest to separate, as all one can
say in individual cases is that the chant is not encountered

with in any other country. The liturgical place of the chant may support this statement. For example, as one of the characteristics of the Esztergom liturgy, on each day of the week before Christmas, the weekday antiphon was ousted by a festive chant which has so far only been found in Hungarian sources:

Antiphonale Strigoniense, Bratislava, Archiv Mesta, EC Lad 2. f 23ᵛ

Di - ci - te: pu-sil - la - ni-mes, con-for-ta - mi - ni, et no - li - te ti - me - re, ec - ce De - us no - ster ve - ni - et et sal - va - bit nos.

(Say: Ye of little faith, gather strength and have no fear! Lo, our God comes and liberates us.)

Similarly, there are several antiphons, responsories and mass Alleluias which are in all probability Hungarian compositions. Their number is not large, but together with local variants and the selection of regional material, they contributed to the singer being able to express his belonging to Europe and also his own native land ("consuetudo hujus patriae").

This is particularly true in the case of chants composed in honour of the country's patron saints. The history of these series of chants also reflects the political and cultural events that took place between 1000 and 1300.

Offices of Hungarian Saints

After the death of King Stephen (1038), the foundations he had laid fell immediately into jeopardy. Debates over succession (Imre, the saintly son of Stephen having died young), a rebellion demanding the restoration of paganism, the martyrdom of many of the bishops, and domestic quarrels fought with foreign help all threatened to destroy internal order and a hardly won independence. Nevertheless, the country surmounted all these difficulties, and by the end of the eleventh century, during the reign of King Ladislas, the saint (1077–1095) there began an almost unbroken period of development lasting 150 years, and elevating Hungary to a great power in Central Europe. This order justly looked upon Stephen, "the saint king" as its founder. When King Stephen and his son Imre, as well as Gerald, the bishop martyr, who did so much for the evangelization of the Hungarians, were canonized in 1083, this provided the opportunity for the first antiphons, in rhymed prose, in honour of Stephen.

Antiphonale Strigoniense, Esztergom, Cathedral Library,
Mss. I. 3. f 6.

A - ve   be - a - te rex Stephane, incli - ta   spes gentis   tu - ae,

a - ve do - ctor et a - pos-to - le credu-li - ta - tis no - strae,

a -   ve spe - cu -lum sancti - ta - tis   et   justi - ti - ae. . .

(Hail, blessed King Stephen, noble hope of your people.
Hail, teacher and apostle of our faith.
Hail, mirror of holiness and pure life ...)

The antiphons that followed early in the twelfth century were now in verse form, according to the fashion of the day:

Antiphonale Strigoniense, Esztergom, Cathedral Library,
Mss. I. 3. f 17.

(St Stephen ascends to the heavenly palace in the height, being elevated from the mortal destiny of our first parents.)

After warring with Byzantium, Hungarian history by the second half of the twelfth century, was perhaps at its zenith. The peaceful reign of King Béla III brought prosperity and a policy of European horizons, also creating suitable cultural conditions. Hungarian literature, arts and music were stimulated by a strong Italian and French influence. Béla III sent his court clerk to Paris to study the new sequence style. French culture was also spread by Hungarian students who studied at Paris university, and by priests and laymen coming from France. The prestige of the Esztergom archdiocese also reached its apogee at the time. Highly cultured archbishops inspired building activity, scholarship and learning, and the reform of the Esztergom liturgy. These, together with the notation of the Esztergom melodic variants, all expressed a reinvigorated consciousness and sense of identity.

It is no accident that it was Béla III who instigated the canonization of his predecessor, St Ladislaus, the knightly king (*athleta patriae*). Typically, the hymns, sequences and office written in honour of King Ladislaus show the influence of the new Parisian melodic style. A fine *contrafactum* to the melody of the famous Holy Cross Se-

quence by Adam of St Victor (an Augustinian canon of
Paris who died in 1192), which was written down on
parchment late in the twelfth century, also dates from this
time:

Pray Codex, f 101.

> *"You became a wondrous mother, virgin, you bore God, there is
> no one like you, with a branch, a flower and an offspring.
> Whoever asks you in true mind, even if tortured by a fatal cross,
> he is granted true salvation in your name. We who stand here in
> your praise, O Mary, listen to us, and lest we fall in the captivity
> of sin, let your entreaty take your servants into the palace of
> your son. Into the house where you reign, bedecked with stars,
> draw us there, too, O blessed one, so that we can honour you
> untiringly, and arrive, in company of the just, to eternal joy.*

Early in the thirteenth century, the vying for a new equilibrium between the four centres of power (king, church, aristocracy and nobility) sparked off inevitable tensions. Impending disaster from without also prevented these restless decades from following their own inner logic and reshaping the country's life. In 1241, the Mongol hordes of Batu Khan invaded the country, they burned down and destroyed everything in their path, decimating the population and dragging them away with them when they withdrew in 1243. The country was left in ruins, with poverty and the fear that the Mongols would return. Internal conflict and moral depravation prevailed until the end of the century, and the dying out of the Árpád dynasty (in 1301). A renaissance came only in the fourteenth century.

New offices written around 1270 gave some comfort and reassurance to the country. The chastity of Prince Imre described in the office in his honour served as a warning against moral depravity. And the new, fully versified office to King Stephen extolled the strength of Christian discipline is superior to all forms of licence. This office is an outstanding work of Hungarian culture of the age of the Árpáds, both as literature and as music.

Antiphonale Strigoniense, Esztergom, Cathedral Library
Mss I. 3. f 11.

Nam ut Athi - la sub re - ge Hunga - ro - rum po - pu-lus ty - ran - ni - dis la - ta le - ge sae - vit in - cre - du - lus, sic sub Ste - pha - no reg - nan - te verti - tur crude - li - tas,

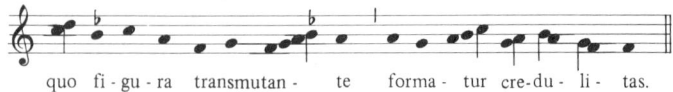

quo fi - gu - ra transmutan -   te   forma - tur cre-du - li - tas.

*(As the people of the Magyars had raged cruelly
during the reign of Attila, following a tyrannical law,
so cruelty changed under the reign of Stephen,
and having changed, devoutness developed.)*

The Esztergom Notation

Musical notation in the Middle Ages was not merely a
device for transmitting music but also provided the most
graphic picture possible of the standard of musical culture,
its articulation and orientation – at least concerning those
fields of music which the man of the day considered to be
important enough to commit to paper.

Hungarian singers became acquainted with notation in
the form known as German Neumes. All that has survived
from the eleventh century are fragments or short musical
inscriptions. Accordingly, the first decades saw the introduction of several varieties of this form of notation in the
country. But records from the twelfth century already point
to a uniform notation, with notators being trained in Hungarian scriptoria which influenced each other and unified
their style. The most considerable relic from this period is
the *Codex Albensis*, an antiphonal of nearly 400 pages
from the first half of the twelfth century. It already shows
typically Hungarian elements of the liturgical and Gregorian tradition, and includes the first Hungarian compositions.

Meanwhile, however, new endeavours emerged in the
most progressive church centres of Western Europe:
Guido d'Arezzo's staff notation was introduced in an un-

changed or a modified form, which enabled musical notation not only to remind the singer of melodies already known to him, but to set down clearly pitches and intervals. Not all forms of neumatic notation were suited to be written on lines, and so all the scriptoria were faced with a difficult decision–if they took note at all of the new, modern principles of notation.

In Hungary, the first signs of experimentation with the use of the new principles appeared in the first half of the twelfth century, and two sources from the end of the century (a fragment and the *Pray Codex*, a sacramentary of great importance both for the history of language and liturgy, dating from around 1192–95) show the new Hungarian staff notation in a fully developed form.

Its origins of course can be traced back to Guido. Still, Guido's notation was not compatible with the tradition of Hungarian musical notation, as it could only have been introduced by totally abandoning the earlier Hungarian practice. German neume notation, on the other hand, was not suited in its original form to mark exact pitches and intervals. The Hungarian scribes therefore adapted French and Italian neume forms for their use, which they evolved in the spirit of the earlier tradition into a new uniform system of signs and technique. The elements of the new notation have several roots, but in its effect the notation is far from being eclectic as it is unified by consistent principles. Upward-bending melodic figures progress forward on the parchment, and are always drawn in unbroken curves, while those bending downwards are placed vertically, and if they consist of more than two notes, feature as separated dots. In combination these two principles can condense long figures, even those consisting of 6 to 8 notes, into a single sign, in which the graphic character, the symmetry and the direction of the notation all ensure legibility and a uniform visual style.

Elementary signs:

Compound signs: etc.

The new notation could be placed on lines without any difficulty, and it marked the pitch exactly. Its introduction naturally entailed huge changes: thousands of melodies had to be deciphered and transcribed, as local melodic variants and notation techniques meant it was meaningless to just copy foreign scores.

This need to change the old choir books with their outdated notation must have provided an opportunity to codify, as it were, liturgical and musical pecularities that had been maturing over a long period. If this was the case, then a three-fold reform took place around 1160–70, in Esztergom, the town and the period whose achievements and the incentives behind them have already been discussed. It should be noted that the transition to staff notation did not take place simultaneously all over Central Europe. There are records of certain isolated initiatives coming from monasteries as early as the first decades of the twelfth century. Esztergom was the earliest archdiocese province to introduce reform in this region, and create a new, uniform notation over a large area.

Thirteenth century fragments from various parts of the country, and a complete notated missal from the diocese of Kalocsa, presumably written in Zagreb, which at the time belonged to Hungary's ecclesiastical organization bear witness to the dispersal of the Esztergom notation. That it is the radiation of a central initiative is also clear from the fact that it was precisely the western border region which stuck for the longest time to the by that time outdated German neumatic notation.

Throughout Europe the new musical notations were always a product of schools with a musical-theoretical background. This musical theory was the highest level of practical musical theory growing out of elementary instruction, and not necessarily the speculative, arithmetic theory that formed part of the *quadrivium*, the higher division of the seven liberal arts. Nevertheless, even this latter must have been not completely unfamiliar, as one of the relevant text books now preserved in a Vienna library, as used at the Dominican college in Buda.

Secular Minstrels and Instrumental Music

But why was the new notation only used for Gregorian chant? Did nothing else exist, or if so, was it considered not worth noting down? Secular music in Europe at the time was only exceptionally entrusted to notation. It was polyphony which called more urgently for literacy, but this will be discussed in the following chapter.

There are indirect sources informing us of the existence of secular music. Anonymus (the author of a famous medieval *Gesta Hungarorum*) related the chronicle of his nation so that, as he put it, they should not only learn about it from the false tales of peasants and the songs of minstrels. Even so, he often refers to these minstrels in his descriptions, and indeed, when writing of the "songs written by the ancient leaders themselves", it turns out that the narratives were heard in the first-person singular, the form of epic performance well known both in the East and the West. The minstrels who recited the epic stories during the age of the Árpáds (eleventh to thirteenth centuries) were known among the people and at the royal court alike, usually as obligatory entertainers at feasts. Documents also show that the new power did not ban the practice of ancient minstrelsy, indeed, it even retained the old name for them (*regös*) and settled them into "regös villages". Their themes might have changed, including the battles and legendary deeds of kings, but the traditional elements of the text and the performing manner of the minstrels lived on throughout the Middle Ages.

Personal names and place-names in documents are supplementary sources in another respect as well. Village names point to settlement of musicians who served at the royal court: wind players and percussionists playing at parades, ceremonies and military events (horn, drum, pipe), singers and instrumentalists who provided entertainment music at feasts, and finally, the epic minstrels. These names do not always mean professional musicians. As in today's village life, workers on the land who play some instrument or other are hired to play music at weddings or balls, so too in the Middle Ages, farming families were ready, for instance at royal command, to serve their masters with music from time to time.

Foreign musicians also turned up at the royal and aristocratic courts as itinerant musicians or in the retinue of visiting lords. Several troubadours and Minnesingers are known to have spent varying amounts of time at the Hungarian royal court (Gaucelm Faidit, Peire Vidal, Friedrich von Hausen, Neidhart von Reuenthal, Walther von der Vogelweide). Although they had no direct effect on Hungarian music, nor were they influenced by Hungarian music, their stay in Hungary still betokens a climate at the royal court which called for the kind of secular lyrical music the troubadours represented.

Record available only advise us of courtly musical customs. The popular practice of minsterly is mentioned chiefly by chroniclers. Early sources refer to the comings and goings of entertainers and itinerant musicians mostly in prohibitory terms, like orders from the synod forbidding principally priests, from receiving or listening joculators and jongleurs, mainly because of the rude, or scurrilous motifs they included in their performances.

Echoes of Folk-music

How can records concerning folk music supplement the musicless music history of the previous section?

We have already mentioned how the words of ancient regölés (greetings) took on new, Christian, in part legendary elements, and how its music approached the simplest patterns of the medieval rondeau. It should also be known that the cultivated songs of the troubadours and Minnesingers in Western Europe also have in their background forms and melodic types of an undocumented common poetry. These can only be inferred from certain accidental notations, songs inserted into liturgical plays, polyphonic arrangements or stylized elite music. Memories of this early secular current music were perhaps mostly preserved by folk music.

Kodály, for example, quotes the following Hungarian dawn song as a relative of a thirteenth century Spanish "alba" song:

CMPH III/A, No. 6.

Ne a - ludj el két sze- mem-nek vi - lá - ga,

Mert majd fel - kel pi-ros haj - nal csil - la - ga.

(Do not fall asleep, light of my two eyes, for the red morning star will rise.)

A fairly close relative of the *conductus* which introduces the queen in the famous French Daniel miracle play, has emerged in a folk wedding tune in Hungary. The Gregorian character of the song which accompanies the folk cus-

toms of Midsummer night might not imply a direct borrowing, it perhaps rather grew from the soil of Old European custom music, related to Gregorian chant. Nevertheless, a harvest song exists, quoted by Kodály, which is a
real Gregorian melody that has passed into secular use:

CMPH II, No. 309.

El- vé- gez-tük, el-vé-gez-tük   az a - ra-tást, az a - ra- tást.

Al - le - lu - ja,   al - le - lu - ja,   al - le - lu - ja.

(We have gathered in, gathered in the harvest, the harvest.)

3 The Late Middle Ages
(14th–15th Centuries)

In 1483, Bishop Bartolomeo de Maraschi of the city of Castello, previously the conductor of the papal choir, came to Buda on a diplomatic mission. In his envoy communique he wrote that King Matthias "has a choir the better of which I have not yet seen. It resembles the one we had (at the papal court) before the devastation of the plague." When "he (the king) had a high mass sung in his chapel ... I had to realize with embarrassment that they have surpassed us in the things that belong to divine worship." At the same period Galeotto Marzio, a friend and biographer of the king, reported that musicians and harpists ate at the king's table, and "they sing the deeds of heroes in their mother tongue, with lute accompaniment, while feasting ... They always sing about famous feat, and there is no lack of these, as Hungary is situated among enemies speaking different languages ... Hungarians–whether nobles or peasants–use almost the same locution and speak similarly ... and from this it follows that a poem written in Hungarian is understood by peasants and burghers, nobles and aristocrats alike."

After the Mongol invasion, the ensuing domestic political disturbances, the dying out of the male line of the Árpád dynasty (1301) and the struggles over succession that followed, Neapolitan Angevins, related to the House of Árpád, acceded to the throne. Their reign opened a period of domestic stability and rapid development in Hungarian history. The external conditions in which this took place were the reigns of two talented and long-lived kings

(Charles Robert 1308–1342 and Louis I., The Great, 1342–1382). Internally there was a differentiation and relative balance of forces within society (the strengthening of towns and the suppression of private aristocratic power), the advance of commerce and mining, a purposeful development of monetary policy, the modernization of the economic structure, comprehensive political and cultural foreign relations, and a sensitive harmonization with new scientific and artistic developments (shown, for example, by the development of higher education, large-scale construction projects of palaces and churches, and more recently by the group of Gothic statues unearthed during excavations in the Buda castle.)

The changes added new colours to the country's cultural map. The intellectual centres–the royal court with its Europe-oriented way of life, initiatives begun by prelates and some barons who modelled themselves on the court, and the church with its growing numbers of highly cultivated clerics–started to bear the fruit of the seeds that had been sown three centuries before. To these may be added new factors, the presence of the Franciscan and Dominican orders (which had entered the country in the thirteenth century and now witnessed a sudden development), and the rich, confident new burgher towns, together with the various institutions and fraternities of the intelligentsia. The effect of urban and village schools in transmitting culture made the map of intellectual life denser and more comprehensive. The new potential of mining and commerce opened up new vistas before the towns along the border region of the Carpathian Basin (Pozsony /Bratislava/, the northern mining towns, the north eastern towns Eperjes /Presov/, Bártfa /Bardejov/, Kassa /Kosice/, and the Transylvanian towns Brassó /Brasov/, Nagyszeben /Sibin/, Kolozsvár /Cluj-Napoca/). This meant that the traditionally well developed central territories were now joined by new towns, partly with a mixed population (Hungarians, Germans and Slavs to the north and Hungarians and Saxons in Transylvania) which were more receptive to neighbouring influences and fashions.

This development that began in the fourteenth century was continued during the reign of King Sigismund of Luxemburg, who was later elected Holy Roman Emperor (1387–1437). Despite the threatening advance of the Ottoman Turks from the Balkans, the fifteenth century brought a further growth in the country's wealth, its regional political influence and cultural potential. The point of culmination was reached during the reign of the Hungarian King Matthias (1458–1490), the son of János Hunyadi who had made his name in the battles against the Turks. Matthias was one of the most prestigious monarchs of the period, not just politically, but also as a generous patron of humanist culture. His library of European renown (known as the Corvina Library) and highly cultured court served as a model for the country's prelates and aristocrats.

The generation that came after the death of Matthias witnessed the collapse of the medieval Hungarian kingdom under the disastrous invasion of the Turks.

Musical Life in Towns

It was characteristic of the history of Hungarian music that the new musical culture of the towns and baronial households instead of replacing the traditional style, rather stimulated it. Towards new growth, ever new elements being added to it without any difficulty. Citizens in the towns played an increasing role in the maintenance and development of church music. Many funds were set up to provide the necessary finances for the musical embellishment of high mass and daily mass. The musical standards in schools are evidenced by the fact that four or five children, led by an adult sufficed for a votive mass, and that they not only sang the regular music of the mass but various musical additions as well, sung in one or more voices.

Various municipal and private records show that the links between burghers and school students were strengthened through the students taking part in the life of the town by singing at receptions of notabilities, on name days, at weddings, on the election of the town mayor, and announcing in song the approach of major holidays, all, of course, for remuneration ("recordatio"). Fifteenth and sixteenth century records go into some detail and show that these services were performed more and more often. Even in small towns and villages, they sang "figuraliter", that is in polyphony. These special events helped the formation of ensembles of proficient singers without, however, shattering what remained a valid basic principle up until the seventeenth century–namely that at high mass the choir was tantamount to the congregation consisting of the whole church and school personnel, and the students as a body. Liturgical singing for 2-3 hours a day, formed an organic part of the intellectual way of life, the extra performances of selected singers only supplementing and colouring this basic layer.

The Organ

The church organ became an important element in the musical life of town dwellers. There are continuous record concerning the building and improvement of organs from the fourteenth century onwards. As well as organs for cathedrals, most frequent mention is made of the building of organs for the new great commercial towns. Medieval records particularly emphasize the organ-building activities of the members of the Hungarian-found Paulite order (a religious order founded in Hungary in 1263) and their skill in playing the instrument.

➤ It is difficult to form a picture of the organists' repertoire. In all probability they would perform (extemporise) harmonic progressions and preludes decorated with figurations, possibly in simple polyphony, such as the one in the only surviving notated example, a Franciscan notation from the fifteenth century. But the "alternating" manner of performance offered them the wide scope. Service books and ceremonial prescriptions often contain the instruction that some of the important sections are to be performed with the alternation of singing and an instrument, exceptionally saying "tangitur in organo", on the organ. Today it cannot be established whether this meant only the playing of the melody, perhaps with instrumental figurations, or whether we can speak of composed, polyphonic versets as early as this. In any case, it is interesting that echoes of this alternating practice is served in twentieth century folk music. The Christmas greetings sung by lads in Transylvania include an accompanying musician who plays. The lads sing their old song, perhaps medieval in origin, in *alternation* with its instrumental performance.

Instruments and Instrumentalists

Choristers selected for special tasks must certainly have included some who were interested in playing instruments. There are records from the turn of the fifteenth and sixteenth centuries of students learning or teaching the clavichord, or a priest leaving his clavichord to his nephews, and so on.

But the rapid growth of instrumental practice in the late Middle Ages catered for replacements from the younger generation chiefly in a guild-like fashion. Here the situation varied from instrument to instrument. The position

of the brass and percussion was already established in the
age of the Árpáds. Their main role was to lend splendour
to the surroundings of the king and the barons on festive
occasions: processions, weddings, coronations, hunting
and of course during wars. Their fanfares, handed down
traditionally from generation to generation within the guild
and about which we have no detailed information must
have reflected the eminence of their lords as much as did
their appearance. They feature in descriptions of one of
King Sigismund's visits abroad, of the meeting between
King Matthias and King Ladislaus Jagello of Bohemia,
and of the coronation of Beatrix, queen to King Matthias.
They were organized and paid in the traditional manner:
divided up into units of a military character, they drew
their livelihood from the villages they had been donated,
borne out by village place-names like Drummer, Horn-
player, etc. But instrumentalists are also mentioned in municipal employment, where they provided music for
marches and processions. For three centuries, from the late
fifteenth century onwards, "royal boroughs" enjoyed the
privilege of employing tower musicians as signallers, fire
watchmen, and to play at festivals.

Another group of musicians, those who played string
and woodwind instruments (violinists, pipers, hurdy-
gurdy-players, bagpipers) are mainly known in medieval
records from personal names signifying occupations. They
are the musicians of the palaces, who provided music for
feasts and domestic festivities. Some of them may also
have been epic minstrels, and others jongleurs, thus making up a heterogeneous group both socially and artistically.
The strolling fiddlers, on a level with the jongleurs, had
the lowest standing, followed by the bagpipers perhaps
setting the mood for a burgher feast and at the top members
of an ensemble playing polyphonic music, for instance to
entertain the queen. Each of these strata features in nar-

ratives, documents, decrees and account-books of the period, but the music they played has not survived in any of their cases.

Apart from organists, it was lutenists who constituted the elite among instrumentalists. From the fifteenth century onwards they figure among tax-paying small-holders and burghers, and in their musical cultivation, fame and independent livelihood they approach the closest to the modern professional musician.

It seems pertinent here to mention *Bálint Bakfark*, even though most of his activity falls into the mid-sixteenth century. Bakfark was born early in the sixteenth century (probably in 1507) in Transylvania. He belonged to the entourage of Voivode János Zápolya of Transylvania, who from 1526 was king of Hungary. Bakfark was about thirty years old when, after Zápolya's death, he went abroad, and won European fame both as a lutenist and as a composer (his music was published in two tablature books). He thus acquired his instrumental training while still in Hungary, among the musicians of the voivode of Transylvania. His instrumental accomplishment and erudition are reflected in his works: lute transcriptions of some of the best polyphonic vocal pieces of his time and free compositions (fantasias), exploiting the potentials inherent in the lute.

Bakfark, B.: Fantasia VII 4 vocum, Opera omnia II/No. 23.

After 25 successful years abroad, Bakfark returned to his native country to spend a few years in Transylvania. But soon he set out again, his life ending in Padua in 1576. According to a Polish adage, the summit of daring is "to turn to the lute after Bakfark". But Bakfark was not the only master of his instrument in Hungary, as borne out by his anonymous teachers in Transylvania and also the lute playing of Hans Neusiedler from Pozsony (Bratislava), whose collections appeared in 1536, 1540 and 1544.

The Royal Court

It was at the Royal court at Buda that the best music of the period was performed and encouraged. We have no data on the music of the century of the Angevin kings and can only draw some conclusions from what remains of other arts in Buda. King Sigismund's interest in music is reflected in his maintaining a close contact with Oswald von Wolkenstein. It is during his reign that we first hear of the choir of the royal chapel and its Hungarian choirmaster. Later records, from the time of King Matthias, also tell of the composition of the choir, its repertoire and high standard. By that time the choir consisted of about 40 members and included, besides singers from abroad, children singing treble. They sang French (Burgundian), Netherlandish and Italian polyphony (obviously alongside plainsong) and according to foreign visitors, their performance rivalled that of the Burgundy court choir and the papal choir.

The standard of court music showed no decline after the death of Matthias, as is indicated by noted singers, composers and conductors entering its service from abroad, further enhancing its reputation (Stockem, Verjus, Lapicida, Stoltzer). This broad European orientation of court music served as a model for the king's humanist clergy. And even though the battle of Mohács in 1526 put an abrupt end to the promise of these high-standard musicians in Hungary, the standards they et were to remain the model for many decades in organizing musical life at the princely court of Transylvania.

Polyphony

Nothing has survived with musical notation of the polyphonic music performed in Buda and the major centres
that modelled themselves on it. This is not surprising since
it was the towns with long-standing traditions (Buda, Esztergom, Pécs, Várad, Veszprém, Eger) that fell victim to
the Turkish ravages. But if the traces of polyphony that
survive from other places are anything to go by, we can
say that in all probability the typical polyphonic forms
were not those of the music cultivated in the great humanist centres. We have two fragmentary yet fairly lengthy
manuscripts of polyphony from the fifteenth century (both
from North Eastern Hungary), and some fragments of one
or two folios from the fourteenth and fifteenth centuries.
The most eloquent sources however are the notated inser-
tions in liturgical manuscripts to supplementing Gregorian
plainsong, constituting vivid and characteristic collection.

These sources include cathedral choir books, collections
used by societies of educated laymen in towns, liturgical
books used in small towns and villages, and monastic antiphonals. The various kinds and styles of polyphonic music
are not evenly distributed in the various sources. The most
generally known form, used both in cathedrals and village
churches seems to have been a two or three part unrhyth-
micized "organal" treatment of plainchant. This archaic
style was probably known for some time before it was
noted down in the fifteenth century (as elsewhere in Europe as well), since it was easy enough and sufficiently
widely practised for the performers not to need written
music. One sketchy form of notation, surviving from a
village area was clearly just a mnemonic. Most of this
music was sung by soloists including two or three part
readings, Passions, gospels, and exceptionally a few choral
pieces as well.

Christmas reading, Antiphonal Zagrabiense, Zagreb, Bibl. Univ.
MR 10. f 147.

(The Lord God says: Return to me, and you shall be liberated.)

Their technique is barely exceeeded by a few rhythmicized tropes and chorales with interchanging parts. Some of them at this period are only found in Hungarian sources, which means that they are possibly Hungarian compositions. The majority are also part of a basic current repertoire found throughout the country.

Graduale ecclesiae Pataiensis, Budapest, National Széchényi Library,
Fol. Lat. 3522, f. 133ᵛ

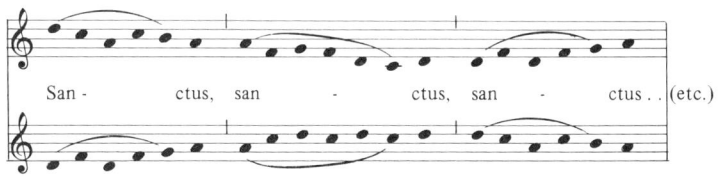

(Holy, holy, holy...)

The next group consists of cantiones, canons and rondelluses more developed rhythmically and in their use of intervals and part writing, but essentially still homophonic. These are generally representative of the central European average (though some of them resemble most closely Italian versions), and even include some unique pieces (e.g. this St Nicholas motet, with a double text). These pieces are not usually written to liturgical texts, nor are they based on a plainchant. They were probably for occasional gettogethers of religious societies and cultured laymen rather than liturgical use.

Fragment from the age of King Sigismund,
National Széchényi Library, Clmae 534.

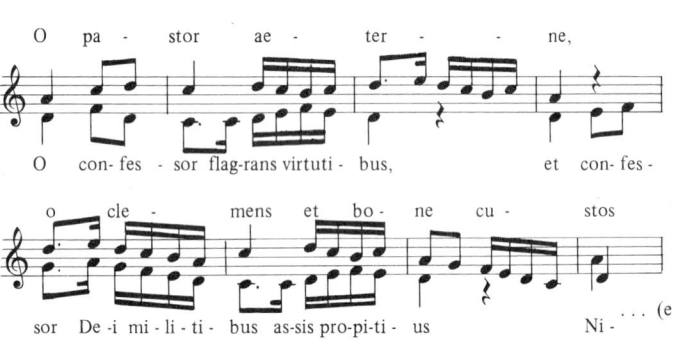

I. Oh eternal shepherd, Oh gracious and kindly guardian...
II. Oh confessor, confessor of God, glowing with merit,
succour mercifully those who struggle...)

The four or five pieces based on a liturgical cantus firmus, but with more complex part-writing we can consider as real compositions. The plainchant in even rhythm sung by the tenor and the more lithe contratenor, are joined by a finely chiseled treble melody animated by ties and syncopation.

Kassa Fragment, Bratislava, provenance unknown.

Ky - ri - e e - le - i - son

(Lord, have mercy upon us...)

Finally there remain a few, fairly isolated pieces which indicate a group of musicians who reflected influences stemming from outside the mainstream. A three-part "Dies est laetitiae" from choir book in Zagreb represents the style of the light homophonic *Gesellschaftslied*, while Frye's "Ave Regina caelorum" (in the Kassa /Kosice/ fragment) shows the presence of Burgundian polyphony and the musical notations in the Brassó (Brasov) choir books that of the imitative style. A fragment discovered some 15 years ago, stemming from a fourteenth century Premonstratensian choir book and recalling the Italian polyphonic style, indicates that more modern polyphony could not have been completely unknown earlier either. These attempts could reflect the increase of music at the humanist court arriving from Burgundy, the Netherlands and Italy.

Absent from this list, however, is the important development in musical history from the thirteenth century onwards: *Ars nova*, the "new art" of Machaut, Ockeghem, Dufay and others. Are the sources perhaps lost? Is it a matter of the distance between the musical regions of the West and the East, or is it possibly a negative Hungarian peculiarity?

I think it is primarily a Hungarian peculiarity. The forms of polyphony listed above can only be cultivated adequately in the same a social soil where plainchant exists. As in content they present a relationship between the main plainchant material and the polyphony that lends colour to it, so too, individually they presuppose a division of roles between the liturgical choir and skilled singers chosen from that choir. This formula is the natural expansion of the system of institutions established in the age of the Árpáds. On the other hand, Western European musical development was in the hands, or rather the minds of professional musicians–musicians known by name. These musicians earned their living in the climate of a network of populous towns, a concentrated university intelligentsia and advanced forms of patronage by princes, aristocrats and the church. Such a reorganization of the Hungarian musical scene had been prepared for by the court chapel at Buda. The boys singing treble might have opted for a musical career that would have ensured them an independent livelihood. Instead, as was to happen so often in later centuries, the course of Hungarian history was determined not by its own inner logic, but by drastic interference from outside.

Plainchant in the Late Middle Ages

The unusual situation and development of modern European art music in Hungary might have been due to another Hungarian peculiarity: the broad basis of a monophonic art. Gregorian chant both as living music and the means of transmitting musical knowledge, not only continued without a break up to the mid-sixteenth centuries (in some places even longer), but in the fifteenth and sixteenth centuries reached its widest currency both geographically and socially. The dense network of churches and schools was on a level in the villages and the towns, at least as far as basics were concerned: the adherence to the liturgical and musical tradition founded in the twelfth century, the singing of a great part of the liturgy (even in small villages entailing daily sung mass and vespers), and above all the participation of every school child in daily services. The effect of this institutionalized practice on public musical awareness, on the "democratizing" of musical culture, on the general musical "memory" and faculties, and on the vitality of the sung material can hardly be fully appreciated. This would have made especially interesting the encounter of this wide-spread art of plainsong, the new, "professional" polyphony, and the Hungarian vernacular usage which gathered momentum in the fifteenth and sixteenth centuries.

The basic plainsong repertoire shows hardly any changes. Three-quarters of the late medieval sources in the traditional centres are identical with those for the early Middle Ages. An increase can be observed in two respects: from supporting institutions and the extension of the repertoire. Both, in different ways, fit into the "main line" of development in a well-ordered, one may say hierarchical manner.

One characteristic feature is some differentiation in the central kernel of institutions and a considerable increase in the number of institutions. These traditional spheres fit well with one other. The central kernel consists of the sung liturgies of Esztergom and Kalocsa-Zagreb, which in two versions continue the original tradition. This is lent colour and individuality by local variants with greater (e.g. that of Várad) or smaller (e.g. that of Eger) differences marking their identity. Sources belonging to the main group include, for example,the *Esztergom Missale Notatum* (fourteenth century), two antiphonals from Esztergom, four antiphonals from Pozsony, the Buda antiphonal (all from the fifteenth century), a good example of the perpetuation of the Esztergom tradition in the so-called *Bakócz Gradual* (turn of the fifteenth and sixteenth centuries). the antiphonals of Zagreb and Várad (Oradea, fifteenth century), and

codices from minor centres (e.g. graduals from Nyitra
/Nitra/, Gyöngyöspata and Transylvania, dating from the
early sixteenth century).

The towns which began their development in more recent times form an outer sphere, being on the periphery
geographically, and greatly receptive to influences coming
from neighbouring peoples. We find the central kernel here
too, but their relative independence their wealth and ethnic
tinge find expression either in melodic variants in the liturgical arrangement, or again in the sung repertory.
Among them, for instance, are the codices of large commercial towns such as Kassa (Kosice), Kolozsvár (Cluj-
Napoca), the medieval Saxon Brassó (Brasov) and Szeben
(Sibin, fourteenth and fifteenth centuries).

The outermost layer is found in the practice of groups,
mainly religious orders, who were readily welcomed in
Hungary and who gave much to its culture. When it came
to their plainsong, however, they kept consistently apart
adhering to their own customs, and only supplementing
the country's practice (*mos patriae*) with their presence,
without borrowing from it or adding anything of their own
to it. Important among these were the Franciscans and the
Dominicans with their considerable literary activity. (Interestingly, the chapel of King Matthias did not follow
Hungarian plainsong practice but used the Italian variety
represented by the Franciscans.)

This means that many new elements emerged without
either breaking the line of tradition, or merging with it.

The same is true for the sung repertoire. In Hungary the
new European styles (late medieval alleluias, chants from
ordinaries, offices to particular saints) were incorporated
and even imitated.

Ferenc Futaki's Gradual, Istanbul, Topkapi Serai,
2429. f 203ᵛ

Alleluja . . . Spre - - vit tho - rum

con-ju - ga ga - lem, in - trat cho - rum vir - gi - na - lem

con - fes - sor Christi, E - me - ri - cus,

Ste - pha - ni re - gis u - - ni - cus . . . (etc.)

*(Alleluia... Having renounced the nuptial bed,
Imre, the only son of King Stephen, the confessor
of Christ enters the host of virgins...)*

These, however, did not dislodge the old repertoire, which firmly held its own. Their incidental role is also apparent from their *ad libitum* character. The examples of current fifteenth and sixteenth century chants which were included in, or indeed omitted from a codex, reflected the tastes and interests of the commisioner or the scriptor of the codex, and not a widespread practice.

Notation

The history of musical notation in the late Middle Ages gives us a graphic impression of the stability, dissemination and differentiation of this plainchant culture. The twelfth century Esztergom notation which evolved out of the reciprocal effect of early Hungarian tradition and modern needs, proved to be fit for further development in these centuries as well. But its changes of form can only be evaluated against the background of the new notations that appeared in the fourteenth and fifteenth centuries.

The religious orders, which kept most detached from the "main line" of Hungarian music stood the farthest apart from the Hungarian dioceses in their musical notation as well. The Franciscans, Dominicans and Carthusians used *square notation*, and in the fourteenth and fifteenth centuries this was used also by the Benedictines and partly the Cistercians (who applied it as an alternative to their notation of Middle French origin). The typical national notation of the *Bohemians* also appears sporadically in towns along the border region, where the musical material itself was of a peripheric character. Also in the border regions, in the north-west, the north and the region of the Transylvanian Saxons, there appeared the most important Central European notation known as the *Messine-Gothic* notation. One of its characteristics is that it does not use the vertically arranged neume signs, and so each note heard later in time appears on the parchment to the right of the previous sign. Besides its conceptual advantages, this also had a technical advantage, as it made it easier for professional scriptors to set out the large-size notes in the ornamental codices which were, in keeping with the taste of the day, in a large format.

In Hungary, however, notation practice divided into two branches in the late Middle Ages. On the one hand, the new demand for large-size, representative chant-books became reinforced when the humanist prelates wanted to perpetuate the practice of their own church in de luxe codices. The original, drawing-like form of Hungarian notation was no longer suited to meet this requirement, and was only insisted on by some of the more conservative institutions (for instance the Pauline order). It needed tradition-bound workshops, which were at the same time perceptive to new demands, to rework Hungarian notation in the spirit of Messine-gothic notation, and bring about a practical, finely shaped, modern yet traditional *mixed notation*.

At the same time, the wide prevalence of musical culture also gave rise to the need for a smaller, cursive personal notation, intended for everyday use. This demand was best met, apart from a few small changes springing from the cursive technique, by the actual original form of Hungarian notation. This cursive Hungarian notation features in very many personal notations from the fifteenth and sixteenth centuries and in more modest choir books copied by non-professional notators for small parishes. One of the interesting documents of this notation is a musical textbook written down by a schoolboy in the late fifteenth century (by László Szalkai, later archbishop of Esztergom). The book, of about 70 pages, contains the basic theory used in general music education, concerning scale systems, notation, intervals, accidentals and modes. The text includes several hundred music examples in a shorthand using Hungarian notation and bespeaking a skilful well-practiced hand. What lends special significance to the book is that, contrary to most contemporary tracts, it does not come from an expert musician, teacher or theoretician, but is a copy made by a 13 or 14 years old boy for his own use.

Two lessons can be drawn from all this. This series of different notations ranging from Hungarian notation to the square notation, exactly corresponds to the late medieval conditions of a system of differentiated but regularly co-existing traditions. And the pattern of Hungarian notation–the duality of representative choir books and what remains in cursive script–reflects the lively, firm and at the same time "democratic" nature of the Hungarian plainsong tradition. This conservativism does have its drawback, but traditionalism and democratization were conditional upon each other.

The Congregational Hymn

But did Gregorian chant, and linked to it, polyphonic Latin hymns fill the framework of church music so fully that it left no room for singing in vernacular Hungarian, that is singing by the people?

First of all, the idea that singing in Hungarian equals the people does not stand the test. There are indications that sometimes the people took part in Latin singing, while at the same time singing in the native language did not only originate as the vocal practice of the people and perhaps not even mainly so. Students singing on town occasions, devout societies, and some nunneries, all supported and also enlarged the repertory of chants in the vernacular, as did the priests and monks active in ministering to the people.

A glance at surviving records shows us that the earliest Hungarian poem is a free translation of the famous Lament of the Blessed Virgin Mary ("Planctus ante nescia"). It is not certain whether the Hungarian version was meant for vocal performance, if so, it was intended not for the people but for students or clergy. Five musical notations with Hungarian words survive from the late Middle Ages: the full Hungarian version of the "Te Deum" (noted down early in the sixteenth century but obviously based on an earlier tradition), three strophic chorales (one of them, "Ave hierarchie", also known abroad, being in all certainty a popular hymn), and a little playful dialogue referring to a liturgical melody. This meagre repertory is supplemented by text notations without any music, which can with great certainty be applied to melodies based on later sources parallels in folk-music and foreign music. Finally retrospective sources are also most useful in this respect: songs which can be dated to the Middle Ages preserved in sixteenth and seventeenth century hymn books and twentieth century folk music. The repertoire of some 30 to 40 items which can be drawn up in this way allows us to make the following sketch of the situation.

According to some data, by the late Middle Ages some texts of the liturgy took root in the Hungarian vernacular in the practice of the people and certain religious communities. In the case of the "Te Deum" this is a certainty, and it is more or less probable for some hymns, parts of the ordinary funeral antiphons, and possibly the introit of the requiem.

Similarly for the plainsong and polyphonic repertoire, so too there is a basic stock of church songs sung in the mother tongue which was known throughout the Hungarian speaking territory and survived for many centuries in the form of popular hymns. Their regular place was before and after the sermon, during processions, and during devotions outside the liturgy. These consists of pieces from the periphery of the liturgy (e.g. sequences, tropes) in Hungarian translation, adaptations of famous European chorales (e.g. "Christ is erstanden", "Dies est laetitiae", "Puer natus in Betlehem"), and pieces of Latin-Hungarian versification in Hungary (e.g. "Natus est nobis rex gloriae", "Collaudemus hunc Dominum"). Some religious hymn verses, most of them with tunes of plainchant inspiration, may have begun in a narrow circle, but in time became part of the stock material of these hymns. Among these are the hymn to the Virgin Mary written in 1508 by the Franciscan monk András Vásárhelyi ("Glorious Lady of Angels") or the shepherd's song sung by students in their Christmas greetings:

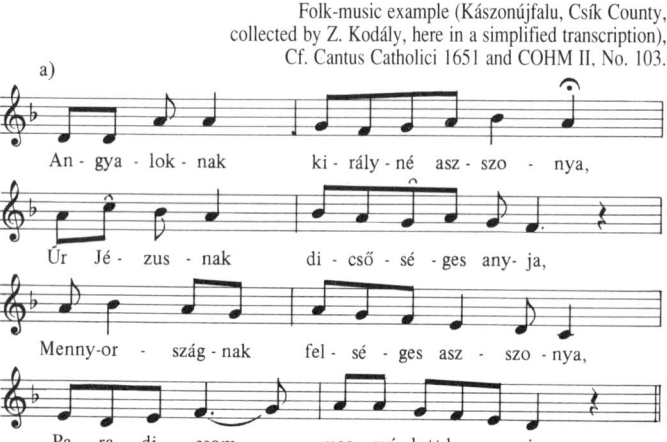

Folk-music example (Kászonújfalu, Csík County,
collected by Z. Kodály, here in a simplified transcription),
Cf. Cantus Catholici 1651 and COHM II, No. 103.

a)

An - gya - lok - nak   ki - rály - né   asz - szo - nya,

Úr   Jé - zus - nak   di - cső - sé - ges   any- ja,

Menny-or - szág - nak   fel - sé - ges   asz - szo - nya,

Pa - ra - di - csom   meg - nyí - lott ka - pu - ja.

(Lady Queen of angels,
glorious mother of our Lord Jesus,
majestic lady of heavens,
gate open to Eden.)

Folk-music example (Hort, Heves County,
Hungarian Academy of Sciences, Folk-music Archives, AP 4560.)
Cf. Cantus Catholici 1651 and COHM II, No. 1.

b)

Csor - da - pász- to - rok   mi - dőn Bet - le - hem - ben,

Csor - dát   ő - ríz - nek   éj - jel   a   me - ző - ben.

(When the herdsmen tended the herd at night in the field at Betlehem...)

A whole range of devout sung poetry on special themes
(e.g. the rules of the religious life), with words in a more
subjective formulation (e.g. lyrical Christmas songs), with
compositions following clerical or monastic requirements

(e.g. hymns of hours) or with a meditative, didactic content (e.g. on the seven words of Christ), were originally written for closed religious communities, and never spread beyond them. Some of them used melodies of well known songs.

This means that the *structure* of the repertoire in the vernacular is not far removed from what we observed in plainsong and polyphony.

Epics

Returning briefly to the musical life of the court of King Matthias, eye witnesses not only described visiting musicians from abroad and the cultivation of Western European polyphonic music, but also the minstrel who stood at Matthias's table and sang of the feats of great Hungarian ancestors, much to the delight of the king, and furthermore in Hungarian, being understood equally by the courtiers and ordinary people.

Heroic epics lived on until the late Middle Ages with listeners among both the higher and lower social circles. This vocal practice based on oral tradition was certainly extemporized, thus naturally being no written records. We know of its existence as mentioned in descriptions of courtly feasts and the celebrations of victorious battles, but it must have been present also in the workaday world, in the same manner as it was found e.g. in the twentieth century in Serbian epics. The kinds of themes can easily be guessed: the history of the Magyar conquest of Hungary, the semi-legendary deeds of glorious kings (for instance St Ladislaus), the deeds of great heroes, and, as we learn from the biographer of King Matthias, by the late Middle Ages episodes from the wars against the Turks also appeared in these songs.

A few poems have come down to us which, even if not perpetuating these traditional heroic epics, presumably

sprang from them: a narrative of a siege, of the death and
memory of a courageous champion, and verse-chronicles
relating the glory of St Ladislaus, the chivalrous Hungarian
king.

We can also deduce the style of their melodies. Since
the ancient lament type of folk-song appeared to be linked
to the sixteenth century epic poem, we are perhaps justified
in thinking that this style, squeezed more or less into
strophes, formed part of the musical vernacular of these
minstrels. One remaining sixteenth century song is derived
from a medieval hymn melody: in this case the epic might
have borrowed its melody from Gregorian chant some 50-
100 years previously. The melody of the hymn of St Ladislaus can be reconstructed on the basis of a sixteenth
century source, itself referring to a third source of inspiration, the repertoire of the semi-professional Western European singers, and their "modes". This melody was certainly widely and regularly sung, and in a really idiomatic
vernacular, as distant variants of it are found in sixteenth
century verse chronicles and twentieth century folk music:

Text: Peer Codex,
melody: Gál Huszár's song book (1560-61),Y₇a.

Csil - la - gok kö - zött fé - nyes - sé - ges csil - lag.

(Hail, gracious King St Ladislas, sweet patron of Hungary,
gracious pearl among the holy kings, a shining star among the stars.)

· Secular Music

We have seen the great help folk-music can provide for an acquaintanceship with congregational hymns and epics, most of which are lost. The only source to turn to is folk-music if we wish to get at least some inkling of the secular vocal customs of medieval society: the repertoire of towns and villages, schools and societies, festivities and games, rural calendar days, and love poetry. Recent analyses of texts, customs and tunes have thrown light on many aspects of this forgotten musical culture. Here we can give only a few examples as an illustration.

The customs of recitation in medieval poetry (including the equivalents of the Meistersingers' modes) are preserved in the verses recited by the best man at weddings, and certain details of folk Nativity plays:

Folk-music example (Gyimesközéplak, Csík County,
Hungarian Academy of Sciences, Folk-music Archives)

Dicsértessék Krisztus, a magos egekben,

ki e ne - mes gaz - dát hoz - ta e - gész - ség - ben . . . (etc.)

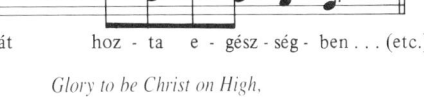

Glory to be Christ on High,
who has granted health to this noble master...)

The nativity play has maintained many other ancient features: cry (*Ruf*)-motifs, songs (songs for (*recordatio*), elements of mystery plays (the existence of which is borne out by old municipal account books and chronicles) and even some remains of dance music.

The cycle of midsummer night (St John's Eve) songs combines medieval ritual, symbolic community games, lyrical love songs and "rivalry" (*certamen*) songs, remnants of old rondeau, and even earlier elements, into a well-arranged sequence:

CMPH II, No. 258/II (Simplified notation).

(Rubato)

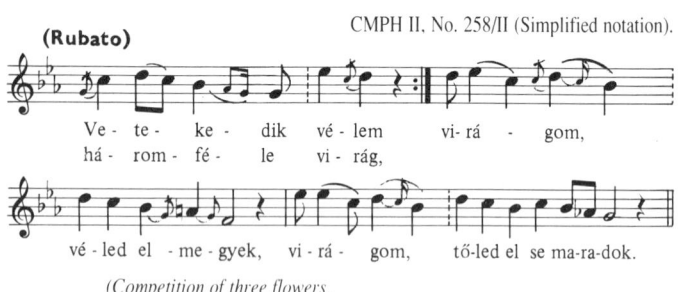

(Competition of three flowers.
Refrain: My flower, with you I will go, my flower, I will not abandon you.)

Folk ballads preserve nearly a hundred types of a genre which may have been introduced by Walloon settlers, becoming Hungarian by assimilation and variation.

One layer of folk-dance music can be traced back to the repertoire of medieval entertainment music: jongleurs and instrumental music for entertainment.

Tápiószecső, Pest County,
Hungarian Academy of Sciences, Folk-music Archives. HMHS p. 564

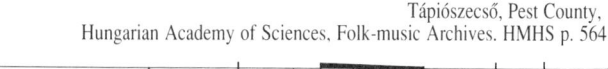

U - tá - na egy pa - ri - pás, a - rany pa - ri - pá - ján.

Állj meg, állj meg, te kis - lány, ad - jál egy kis vi - zet,

Hogy i - tas - sam pa - ri - pám, az - tán meg - ö - lel - lek.

(There goes a young girl, carrying a jug on her shoulder,
a lad follows her on a golden steed.
Stop there, stop there, little girl, give some water
so that I can water my steed, and then I'll embrace you.)

One group of melodies, rich in variations, is made up of free formulations of an underlying European melody, performed sometimes *parlando*, sometimes in the popular *volta* rhythm, and sometimes squeezed into "old" asymmetrical rhythmic elements:

CMPH III/A, No. 272 (simplified notation).

a)

Fel-nyőtt az út mel-lett két szál ma-jo-rán - na,

Nem sze - re - tyi főd-jét, el a - kar búj - dos - nyi,

A nap-tól, a hód - tól bú - csút a - kar veny - nyi.

(Two marjoram plants grow at the roadside,
they don't like their ground, they want to leave
and take leave of the sun and the moon.)

CMPH III/A, No. 259 (simplified notation).

Sír - jál te vi - rág,   no te szűz vi- rág,   most van mi-ért sír - nod!

I- de-gen a- pá-nak,   i- de-gen a-nyának   hol ta-lá-lod ked- vit?

*(Weep, flower, you virgin flower, now you have good reason to cry,
how can you please a step-father, a step-mother?)*

CMPH I, No. 1096.

Für - dik   a   ká   -   csa   fe - ke - te tó   -   ba,

fi - á - hoz ké - szül   Len-gyel-or-szág - ba,   Len-gyel-or-szág - ba.

*(A black duck in a black lake, is about to go
to her son, in Poland, in Poland.)*

Istensegíts, Bukovina, collected by Z.Kodály.
Vargyas, L. Collection of Examples, No. 296.

Most jöt- tem Er - dély-ből   Hat ló - val, hin - tó - val,

Hat ló - val, hin - tó - val,   S egy ron- gyos szol- gá - val.

*(I've just come from Transylvania, with a coach
and six, a coach and six, and a servant in rags.)*

4 The Period of Turkish Occupation

(16th and 17th Centuries)

Three months after the lost battle of Mohács, fought against the Turks in 1526, János (John Zápolya) the Voivode of Transylvania, made his entrance into Buda. The voivode's court chaplain wrote of his first day in Buda: "Since Buda-Pest at the time was destroyed, and only its smoky walls could be seen, many dead bodies were lying everywhere in the streets and squares ... We dined at the hour of vespers. And after we had eaten, voivode János told me: Make preparations, Father György, to sing vespers! Together with chaplain István, we went into the chapel of his royal majesty. The priest there was an honest fellow, Gergely, now broken by age, who had been born in Pest and from his early youth on had a fine voice. We rung the bells once and then twice and at the third peel the castellan had the cannon of Buda castle fired, and many lords and together with voivode János, sang in chorus the vespers for All Saints." Here in a single scene is the farewell to one period and the beginning of another.

For nearly a hundred years, Hungary had tried to resist the onslaught of the Ottoman Turks that threatened the whole of Europe. By 1526 the country's forces, were all spent, and it received no help in the struggle. Hungary lost the Battle of Mohács, and the Turks pressed forward along the course of the Danube, extending the territory under their occupation (Buda fell in 1541). There ensued 150 years of Turkish rule over some two thirds of the country. With some periodic variations, the borders of the occupied territory ran roughly along the line of Lake Balaton to the west, the course of the Danube and the mountain spur to the north, and the central range of the Transylvanian mountains to the east and south.

- The battle of Mohács claimed the life of the king, and the barons were unable to agree as to whether an effective defence against the Turks would best be served by electing a national king (the party on this side had Voivode János Zápolya crowned king) or by the election of Ferdinand of Habsburg who would promote–with Western European help–the expulsion of the Turks. The struggle between the two kings ended in mutual agreement whereby Zápolya and his successors were to return to Transylvania, henceforth given the status of an independent principality, while Ferdinand was left to reign over the western and northern territory free of Turkish occupation. The Habsburg monarch thus became the freely elected king of a Hungary legally independent and only in a personal union with Austria. But during the rule of Ferdinand's successors the Habsburgs strengthened their hold over Hungary, which gradually lost its independence. The separation of "royal Hungary" and Transylvania was never considered in the country to be final. At times Hungary tried to incorporate the principality, while at other times the Transylvanian princes led independence struggles (István Bocskai 1604–1606, Gábor Bethlen 1613–1629 and György Rákóczi I 1630–1648).

- The Turkish occupation and the country's division into three parts brought immense suffering, devastation, depopulation and pauperisation, and retarded the development of a middle-class, driving the country back into a form of agrarian economy based on noblemen's estates with serf labour, a situation unchanged until the nineteenth century. At the same time it led to the atrophy of the forces that supported and stimulated culture, and blocked the maintenance of relations with Europe.

· The spread of Protestantism (approximately from 1540 onwards, but checked by Counter-Reformation in the seventeenth century) also affected the position of culture and music. The network of institutions of the Catholic Church which, because of the Turkish occupation had anyway been reduced to a small area, now became weakened, Calvinism, the branch of Protestantism that prevailed in Hungary, did not found similar institutions, and its ideal of divine service did not require a systematic transmission of musical culture. On the other hand, its intellectual endeavours brought a tremendous impetus to the flowering of literature and monophonic singing in the vernacular.

The Transylvanian Court

After the break in historical continuity caused by 1526, what social forces remained to stimulate the maintenance, and future development of music?

For a time it seemed that some of the liberal minded aristocratic patrons of culture (for example the Nádasdy family) could fulfil this role. But the wars, the absence of an exemplary royal court and the absence of peaceful baronial households prevented the development of artistic patronage. The life of aristocrats engaged in war and superintending their estates demanded a different kind of music: instead of Renaissance or early Baroque instrumental ensembles, they had groups of brass and percussion instruments playing medieval style music, and quieter instruments for table music.

Until the end of the sixteenth century, the musical standards of the former royal court at Buda was most closely approached by the princely court in Transylvania. Zápolya's successors, desirous of imitating this erstwhile royal splendour, both for reasons of prestige and out of a real love of music, brought many foreign instrumentalists to their court, thus also initiating musical connections abroad, mainly with Italy. Of the professional musicians gathered around these princely patrons, G.B. Mosto, the madrigal composer and A. Venetus, an organist, both from Venice, as well as P. Busto of Brescia, are known by name. An organ tablature dedicated to Prince János Zsigmond, son of János Zápolya (Diruta: *Il Transilvano*) and the Palestrina motets dedicated to cardinal Prince András Báthory match the portraits contemporaries drew of these princes, who themselves played the organ. Descriptions of the varied use of music seem to indicate a variety of styles as well. Wind music features in descriptions of national assemblies, parades and banquets, indicating the survival of an earlier type of music, while the church music, vespers and motets played at weddings and on political occasions plus the organ, lute and virginal music in the palace indicates the presence of Renaissance polyphony and instrumental music. Even so, the Transylvanian court was hardly able to exercise a wide influence, and although a growing number of Hungarian names appear in lists of musicians from the seventeenth century, the collections of instruments and reports by chroniclers lead us to conclude that the musical scene in the principality had rather the occasional character of aristocratic "bands" instead of being modelled on early developments in the Italian and German Baroque.

Musical Life in the Towns

The civic towns in the part of the country which remained unoccupied began with a more modest potential where music was concerned, yet it was here that the foundations for the future were laid. The loss of the old towns of great eminence meant that Sopron and Kőszeg on the western border, Pozsony (Bratislava), Nagyszombat (Trnava) and

Körmöcbánya (Kremnica) in the north-west, Eperjes (Presov), Bártfa (Bardejov) and Lőcse (Levoca) in the north-east, and Brassó (Brasov) and Szeben (Sibin) in Transylvania (nearly all Lutheran towns) were in an advantageous position. This was because the conditions for art music there were created not by an aristocratic patron, religious institution or monastic order, but by the urban citizenry and the magistracy themselves.

The students of the chapter school of Esztergom, which had fled to Nagyszombat (Trnava) from the Turks, still participated in the old manner in Gregorian chant and figural singing in church. In the other towns, local dignitaries saw to it that the church should have 4-5 (sometimes more) vocalists, an organist and a choirmaster who, together with children singing descant, performed motets, polyphonic vespers and masses.

Since in most places the same dignitaries had the disposal of both the city's own musicians and the church musicians, works combining instrumental and vocal performance following to stylistic change of the seventeenth century, could also be played in the free royal boroughs by involving the tower musicians. The relative prosperity of certain cities meant these were a larger number of professional musicians, and also applicants could be subject to selection. Better schools also increased the possibility for bolder undertakings. By the mid-seventeenth century, there was no obstacle to the introduction of polychoral technique and early Baroque choral music accompanied by a fairly large orchestra, for example in Sopron and Bártfa.

Beside the records gained from accounts, documents and narratives, sources with musical notation at this time also lend us a better acquaintaceship with the musical scene of the period. The book of polyphonic vespers presented to Pozsony (Bratislava) parish church in 1571, for instance, contains more than 200 antiphons, responsories and hymns for two to six voices, partly by notable foreign composers (Finck, Mouton, etc.), but mostly by unknown (possibly local) composers, arranged in liturgical order.

Pozsony Polyphonic Vesperal, 1571. Bratislava, Chapter Library, Knauz 11. f 51ᵛ

(And they said among themselves: Who shall roll us away the stone...)

Large collections of printed and manuscript volumes and tablatures survive from Bártfa (Bardejov) and Lőcse (Levoca), and the 2,000 pieces featuring in them represent the most important German, Netherlandish, Silesian and, to a lesser extent, Italian composers of the time, as well as some Hungarian composers (e.g. Farkas Greffinger, organist at Buda and later at Brassó /Brasov/). The sources with musical notation clearly show the path which led from the repertoire of Renaissance motets through Venetian concertante and polychoral technique to Schütz, and Baroque works built on a figured bass.

The intertwining of town and church meant not only a larger and more versatile group of musicians being available both for religious and secular occasions (city festivals, reception of illustrious guests, political events, tower music, civic entertainment). By providing a stimulus for the gathering together of professional musicians and ensuring the possibility of fairly stable employment, it created the preconditions for modern musical life. This is true even if the small number of towns concerned and the narrow geographical and cultural region (a band of cca 200 by 800 km, running from west through north to the eastern borders) did not right away allow for the development of a long-due musical confraternity. It is also true that, as a result of circumstances, the musicians included a disproportionately large number of newcomers and non-Hungarian speaking citizens.

Composers

The *regens chori* and/or the organist, who was in charge of the musical life of a town was in most cases also a composer. Apart from Bálint Bakfark, who belongs in a category of his own, Hungarian composers may lie behind the many anonymous pieces in sixteenth century collections. In the seventeenth century the situation improved a little, though still there is more biographical data than actual composers knowable from any surviving works.

Andreas Rauch (1582–1656) came to Sopron from Austria, but his thirty years of activity in Hungary and the works he wrote there turned him into a Hungarian composer. His early works continued the light, slightly polyphonic German secular song repertoire, but the many festive works written for religious and state occasions in Sopron (funeral music, psalms, litanies, "Currus triumphalis") already show the early Baroque style enriched with orchestral accompaniment.

A. Rauch: Musicalisches Stammbüchlein, No. VIII
(Musicalia Danubiana 2, p. 111.)

be - tet, Han - na stund auf und be - tet, Han- na stund auf

auf und be - - tet, Han - na stund auf

Han - na stund auf, Han - na stund auf und be - tet,...(etc.)

Anna got up and prayed like this...)

The active musical life of the schools and churches in Sopron provided work for many other composers as well. János Kusser (1626–1659), born in nearby Ruszt and later active in Pozsony (Bratislava), finally working in Stuttgart as an organist, began his career in Sopron ("Concertum sacrorum quatuor et quinis vocibus..."). Samuel Capricornus (1628–1665) also studied music and played in Sopron, later working in Pozsony (Bratislava), where he wrote several major works to commission (choral pieces, in part with instrumental accompaniment). His nephew and pupil György Strattner (1644–1704), born in Moson County, after his student years in Pozsony (Bratislava) worked as a choirmaster and teacher in Germany (cantatas, stage works). Another Sopron organist was János Wohlmuth (1643–1724), who worked also in Wittenberg and Regensburg (a five-part Miserere with violins and trombones has come down to us).

The surviving motets and Magnificats of the Bártfa organist Z. Zarewutius (1605?–1667) reveal him to be a skilled composer of polychoral homophony.

Z. Zarewutius: Magnificat secundi Toni VI, bars 11-19
(Musicalia Danubiana 8, p. 121.)

(...and now and ever shall be...)

A more animated instrumental and vocal Baroque style found in the same region, for instance in the masses, motets and Magnificats of the Szepes organist Johannes Schimbraczky from Szepesség (Spis), (?–1657) and the organ, preludes, fantasias and chorale preludes of Samuel Marckfelner of Lőcse (Levoca) (1621–1674). Church works by the Lőcse choirmaster János Spielenberg have survived in the János Kájoni collection.

János Kájoni (1629/30–1687) is one of the most interesting and versatile figures in seventeenth century Hungarian music. A Franciscan monk from Transylvania, he studied at Nagyszombat (Trnava), where his intellectual horizons were broadened, his field of interests ranging from botany to organ building. Sharing the same versatility in music, he made a manuscript collection of copies of the best of contemporary Italian church music (e.g. works by Viadana) and also copied medieval Hungarian plainchant manuscripts for his own use. He published the fullest collection of Hungarian Concgregational Hymns for Transylvania (*Cantionale*, 1667), and also noted down secular songs and Hungarian, gipsy and Romanian dances. His own works are pieces of monophonic liturgical music simple in texture and with organ accompaniment.

Kájoni, J.: Litany, in Szabolcsi, B.: A magyar zenetörténet kézikönyve
(Handbook of the History of Hungarian Music),
collection of examples VII/10c: bars 38-50.

ca - ta   mun -   di.   mi - se -   re -   re   no -   bis.
                        par - ce   no - bis   Do - mi -   ne.

(Lamb of God, that takest away the sins of the world,
have mercy upon us, show mercy unto us, Lord.)

Still in Transylvania, during the seventeenth century there worked the Brassó (Brasov) organist, Daniel Corner (1656–1740), whose works illustrate the spread of a more independent Baroque instrumental style, while the music of Gabriel Reilich (1643–1677), who first worked in Pozsony (Bratislava) County, then moved to Beszterce (Bistrita), finally settling in Szeben (Sibin) as organist and court composer to a noble family, marks an ascendancy of the melodic German Baroque song style.

Verse Chronicles

This musical culture existed within a narrow geographical circle, under unfavourable conditions but following European developments. Unfortunately the cultivators of this musical culture were in part isolated examples in the midsts of a quite contrary process, process being a new, rapid ascendancy in Hungary of monophony. It must be said that this monophony no longer formed a part of high art music as did plainsong nor was it an everyday supplementation to the "high concert" of the Middle Ages and its secular monophony. This new monophony, formally simple though perhaps monumental, encompassed by music in its entirety wherever it struck root. Its appearance originated from negative and positive forces. On the one hand, a weakening of the gravitation towards art music, a loosening of direct European links, and the decline of musical cultivation among the higher intellectual layers of society, and on the other the new social role of a flourishing vernacular literature and the increasing importance of singing in shaping political, social and religious consciousness. All this led to an emphasis on monophonic strophic song conveying the textual content in the simplest form. Music, one might say, became the handmaid of occasional (propagative, didactic, entertaining) literature.

Typical examples of this "versification for general use" appeared at the turn of the fifteenth and sixteenth centuries, after 1540 moving to the centre of intellectual life, obtaining a new literary and social function. The number of poems written within just a few years exceeded the whole medieval output many times over. They mostly came from the pens (or rather the lutes), of literate members of the minor intelligentsia, who, mainly due to political and religious developments, had lost their old ground, or rather, gained a new foothold.

The main themes of the poems, which are really verse chronicles, were linked, directly or indirectly, with the most pressing question of the age–the struggle against the Turks. From this came the name chronicle-song style for the whole trend. Narrations of sieges and the deeds of champions in battle inspired firmness and resolve as did parable from the Bible or the historical past. Their moral aims were even more evident in epic songs about virtues and failings, heartening or reproving the listener. Theological polemics, controversial or biting attacks against the other religion also gained ground. The same style was used in entertaining romances and lays, often drawing upon foreign sources, and in instructive songs sung at banquets and weddings, serving direct social needs.

Regarding their form, they are lengthy narratives running to 100 or even 150 strophes, aiming at a graphic, detailed description of the subject rather than the display of poetic skills. Most of them are in four-line strophes, often with a syllable count of 4 x 11 (12 or 15). Sometimes also make use of popular medieval formulae (e.g. the epic line of 4 + 6 syllables), and sometimes employ intricate combinations (e.g. 4 lines of 10, 10, 10, and 11 syllables formed from the "volta" rhythm, long-lines in a triple division of 5 + 5 + 6 syllables, and carefully composed strophes with syllable counts of 6 + 7, 6 + 7, 6 + 6 + 7). The retrospective character of the heroic song is also evident in that it often includes reformulations of medieval or even earlier traditions both in its literary formulation and the musical material (for instance strophic variants of the lament style).

The musical material, too, is subordinated to conveying the long text rather than any independent expressiveness. Unadorned syllabic note progressions in simple metric and rhyhtmic formulae sometimes underline their dependence on the words by a parlando style of performance. The melody avoids large interval steps, and contains many note repetitions or scale progressions which are well adapted to the delivery of the text. In most cases what lends the melodies a convincing strength is the inspiration of the old modes and an almost gloomy dignity, without any show.

The Story of Tobias,
Hofgreff Collection in Régi Magyar Dallamok Tára
(COHM) I. No. 15.

Jer - sze em - lé - kez - zünk mos - tan mi nagy dol - gok - ról,

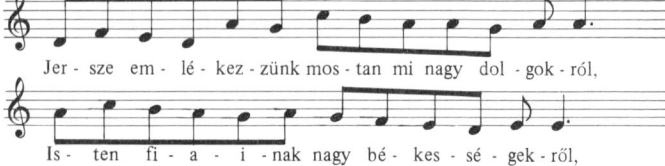

Is - ten fi - a - i - nak nagy bé - kes - sé - gek - ről,

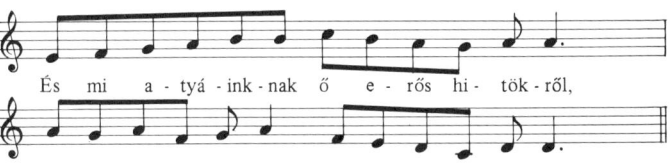

És mi a-tyá-ink-nak ő e-rős hi-tök-ről,

Hogy ne fe-led-kez-zünk so-ha mi e-zek-ről.

(Come, let us now remember the great things, the great peace of the sons of God, and the strong faith of our fathers, let us never forget these.)

Verse chronicle poets sometimes included their name in the initial letters of the lines. From the legion of anonymous authors there emerges one true personality who has proved worthy of his contemporary fame both as regards the literary treatment of his themes and the individual, at times slightly mannered treatment of his melodies, he being the first to be raised to noble rank for his songs. This was Sebestyén Tinódi the Lutenist (cca 1510–1556), whose *Cronica* was printed in Kolozsvár (Cluj-Napoca) in 1554.

Tinódi, S. 'the Lutanist': "The capture of Szitnya, Léva..." in COHM, I, No. 39.

Le-szön be-szé-döm it-ten ez or-szág-ról,

Szit-nya, Lé-va, Csáb-rág, Mu-rány vá-rá-ról,

Fer-di-nánd ki-rál el-ron-ta-tá-sá-ról,

A ben-nök va-lók-nak nagy-szer-nyő ha-lá-lok-ról.

(Here I shall speak now about this country,
about the castles of Szitnya, Léva, Csábrág, Murány,
the defeat of King Ferdinand,
the dreadful death of those in the castle.)

At the same time an anonymous collection of biblical stories was also published in Kolozsvár (Cluj-Napoca), (referred to as the Hofgreff Collection, after the name of the printing house). If Tinódi's *Cronica* is worth attention for its individual style, what makes the latter collection interesting is precisely that it seems to have preserved the heroic song in its typical, customary idiomatic state.

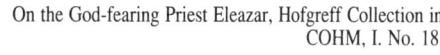

On the God-fearing Priest Eleazar, Hofgreff Collection in
COHM, I. No. 18.

Ré - gen ó - tör-vény- ben   va - la   Je - ru - zsá - lem - ben

egy   ha - tal - mas ki - rály   ő nagy ke-vély - sé - gé - ben,

hogy ki az zsi-dó - kat mind ö - le- ti   va - la   ő nagy keménységében.

(In olden times, in the Old Testament there was a powerful king in Jerusalem, who in his great haughtiness had all the Jews killed with great harshness.)

The two collections preserve altogether 40 melodies. Since some of the verse-chronicles were perpetuated in folk tradition as well, indeed with their original melody, this number can be supplemented by folk tunes as well:

Gyergyai, Albert: On Prince Árgirus.
The melody from folk-music collection in Istensegíts, Bukovina.
Kodály, Z: Retrospection II, p. 80.

Búj- do - sik Ár - gyi - lus he - gye - ken völ - gye - ken,

Er - dőn s kő-szik - lá - kon s ki - et - len he - lye - ken,

Búj - do - sik e - gye - dül csak egy i - na - sá - val,

Kit el - vi - ve ú - ti - tár - sá - nak ma - gá - val.

(Árgirus is wandering over hills and dales, forests and cliffs, in desolated places, he is wandering alone, with a single servant whom he took along as a travel companion.)

Finally the number of heroic songs was considerably increased by many of them being used with sacred texts, thus transferring them into communal use. In this form they have survived both in written form (church hymn-books) and oral tradition (church songs, and funeral wake songs). Melodies of folk hymns were also sometimes borrowed for verse-chronicle texts.

Graduals

This sharing of melodies is not fortuitous. Behind the verse-chronicles and the new church songs lay similar aims and often the same singers.

The Reformation, which gained ground in Hungary around 1530–40, took two paths as far as music was concerned, both being attempted at the outset. One was the use of liturgical music handed down from the Middle Ages, the other was the further development of the medieval *cantio*. It was not evident at first that the two represented two different standpoints one might say two different ideologies, which in a hundred years time would explode into open conflict.

The first move towards church reform was to translate the liturgy into the vernacular. At Székesfehérvár, the mass had been said in Hungarian immediately prior to the Turkish occupation of the town. At Gyulafehérvár (Alba Julia),

the office was sung in Hungarian in the chapter church.
This called for the translation of a considerable part of the
Gregorian liturgical vocal repertoire, facilitated to some
extent by a freer use of the repertoire, abandoning old liturgical restrictions.

A fragment of manuscript dating from around 1542 already includes a Hungarian translation of the Magnificat
and two more Gregorian chants. According to a contemporary record, the Hungarian adaptation of a not incon-
siderable repertoire of melodies was completed within a
few years, or possibly a few months. It seems that several
repertoires must have existed side by side, as a collection
published in 1560 differs from the main tendencies otherwise clearly evidenced in sources from the end of the sixteenth century onwards. Based on the fragment mentioned,
this 'main stream' of tradition can be dated to about 1540.

The number of translated chants comes close to a thousand. The melodic variants and the notation are usually
based on the Hungarian (Esztergom) tradition. The repertory consists of antiphons, hymns, passions and sequences,
while the more elaborate mass chants required by feasts
of the ecclesiastical year (with the exception of a few in-
troits) were supplemented during main service by the easier musical material of the office (hymns and antiphons).

Batthyány Gradual, pp. 183 and 344.

*(And very early in the morning the first day of the week, the women
came unto the sepulchre at the rising of the sun, alleluia.)*

I - me el - jött az u - ral - ko - dó Krisz - tus,

és az or - szág va - gyon az ő ke - zé - ben,

és az ha - ta - lom és az bi - ro - da - lom.

(Lo, Christ the ruler has come,
and the reign is in his hands,
and the power and the realm are too.)

Manuscript copies of the material were made, in increasingly poorer notation, in books called graduals (about twenty of which survived). Since the material of these graduals was not intended to be sung by the congregation but, along medieval lines, was for use by teachers and schoolboys, it did not really need to be printed. The two graduals that appeared in print did so for specific reasons. The gradual of 1574 by the preacher Gál Huszár was intended as a compilation of the liturgical plainsong (including the recitative parts chanted by the celebrant) and the strophic congregational chants. A few decades later, two princes of Transylvania, Gábor Bethlen and György Rákóczi, desiring to unite the Hungarian Calvinist congregation in a High-church type of congregation, spared no expense to further this aim. They commissioned bishops János Keserüi Dajka and István Geleji Katona to prepare an exemplar copy by collecting a great many manuscripts. This was called the *Great Gradual*, and was printed and sent out to all the congregations free of charge (1636).

The manuscripts however were still not fully concordant. For instance in Eperjes (Presov) the local Hungarian Lutheran congregation at the time used a gradual with a completely different repertoire. An interesting feature of this Eperjes Gradual is that it includes not only Gregorian chant in vernacular but congregational hymns as well, often in four parts (accompanied by triadic modal harmony).

But the *Great Gradual* was a belated attempt. By that time a Puritan movement among church leaders was in full swing, opposing liturgical practices that went beyond the preaching of the Gospel. Interestingly, this purifying action, which proclaimed the exclusiveness of singing by the people, met with the opposition of the people. By the mid-century the experiment with graduals came to an end, and during the following two centuries only a few of its elements remained in a few manuscripts.

The end of this experiment coincided with the Catholic Church's decision (executed by Péter Pázmány, the archbishop of Esztergom and the greatest writer of the Counter-Reformation in Hungary) to abandon the tradition of the Hungarian version of Latin plainsong and introduce the reformed Tridentine liturgy. Today it is moving to observe how for still some time to come this musical "mos patriae" sought refuge in poor manuscripts in small villages, before finally falling into silence. Thus by the mid-seventeenth century, the history of six and half centuries the Hungarian of *cantus planus* had come to an end. The only exception was the Romanized plainsong still sung compulsorily in a number of cathedrals and monasteries.

Congregational Singing

"Let us turn the churches into schools!" This programme could be carried out more easily via the strophic congregational hymn developed from the medieval *cantio*. And since this new singing proved to be a tremendous conquering force, the Catholic Church could not resist it: in most church services (excepting some high masses accompanied by polyphonic music and Gregorian plainsong) "congregational singing" had gained pre-eminence in the seventeenth century.

Here too, it was not so much a case of gradual beginnings and a slow growth, but rather the feverish creative work of a few years. The printed Protestant hymn books that appeared after the mid-sixteenth century contained practically the whole repertoire of several hundred songs which was to remain the standard material of congregational singing for many decades.

The oldest layer consists of medieval cantiones: festal songs resting on European or Hungarian traditions. These were supplemented by translations of a few German songs, but the overwhelming majority consisted of original Hungarian verse: poems written after the manner of the verse chronicles, using for the most part its stock of melodies, and interpreting the Scripture, as well as psalm paraphrases and songs of thanksgiving. Although the melodic material drew upon different sources, until the early seventeenth century it preserved a firmly uniform, old style, adapting the borrowed melodies to this as well.

Kolozsvár Song Book, 1744 in COHM I, No. 100/I.

Ó én két sze - me - im, ti az Úr - ra néz - ze - tek,

Hogy ke - gyel-mes hoz- zám min - den- kor, el - higy- gyé - tek.

Az ő nagy szerel-mét, hozzám nagy jóvoltát mindenkor hirdessé - tek.

(Oh, my two eyes, look upon the Lord,
that He is mercyful to me, always believe it,
His great love and his good offices to me you always profess.)

Humanist education was accompanied by the appearance of metrical tunes set to classical verse forms early in the sixteenth century. About fifty of them were published in print by the Brassó (Brasov) teacher Johannes Honterus in 1548. True, they were not long-lived in schools, but some of the more successful melodies found their way, with new words, in among the congregational hymns. In doing so, however, they had to lose their very essence, the scanned rhythm, to be able to mix with the typical parlando-melodic style of the latter.

Cantus Catholici 1651 in COHM, I, No. 138/I.
The metric interpretation of the tune above it
according to Honterus, J.: Odes (1548).
Below it, present-day folk-music recording: Hadikfalva, Bukovina.
Hungarian Academy of Sciences,
Folk-Music Archives, AP 3602/b

(May we continue in true faith all through,
although here on earth we must live in misery...)

The process of assimilation and the emergence of a new style was probably helped by the fact that, apart from Gál Huszár's uninfluential publications, for a hundred years only the texts were published. The long-felt need for a publication with musical notation was first filled by the Catholics, but only in 1651 (*Cantus Catholici*), it took another hundred years for the Calvinists to follow suit (Kolozsvár /Cluj-Napoca/ hymn books 1744, 1777, Debrecen hymn books 1774, 1778). The rigid notations of all these books bear out Kodály's observation: the real, authentic melodic forms were preserved not by these books but by the living memory of the people.

Kolozsvár Song Book, 1744 in COHM I. No. 232/III.
Below it, folk-music recording: Lövéte, Udvarhely,
Hungarian Academy of Sciences, Folk-Music Archives.

(Do not contend with me, O my sweet God, because then my soul cannot be washed of its sins before You, You may condemn me.)

The printed hymn books, together with other publications and manuscripts produced in quick succession by the Catholics, such as Lénárd Szegedi's hymn book (1674), István Illyés's funeral songs (1693), György Náray's *Lyra*

Caelestis (1695), the *Túróci Choral Book* (c. 1700), contained only a reduced number of sixteenth century congregational hymns of homogeneous in style and classic in value. From the seventeenth century onwards, this material became supplemented–and threatened–by new, less and less desirable stylistic trends. The Calvinists took over the body of Geneva psalms in a translation by Albert Szenczi Molnár (1607), which though valuable in themselves were difficult to reconcile with Hungarian traditions and were never really been assimilated. Their propagators actually served to oust the older more organic tradition. At the same time the composition of Catholic repertoire acquired the colour, and the shallowness, of the new German and Italian chorale style which accompanied the Counter-reformation, mainly through the medium of the Jesuits. These new trends encouraged Hungarian dilettantes to write compositions.

Cantus Catholici 1651 in COHM II, No. 200.
Folk-music recording: Lövéte, Udvarhely County,
collected by Forrai, M.

Hic ig - nis fri - get, hic a - mor ri - get, ...

Ó, fé - nyes sze-mem, ha - sadj meg, szí - vem, ...

(Oh, what do I see, what do I view, when I look upon the cross,
upon my dear, crucified Jesus.)
(Oh, my shiny eyes, break my heart...)

The Style of the Seventeenth Century Songs

The change in the style of congregational hymns was parallelled in the secular sphere. It was as though the medieval song, forced underground by the hard times, now surfaced again like an intermittent stream. From the late sixteenth century onwards collections of poetry by the literati were filled with lyrical texts, still usually sung poetry. Love poetry, poems about the pangs of love, outlaws' songs, mocking songs and revellers' songs alternated with soldiers' songs and sometimes even political poems of a more subjective character. Their tunes unfortunately were not written down, as by that time the knowledge of musical notation was confined to a narrow circle, the melodies were either already known or the verses were sung *ad notam*.

A few written sources and again folk memory can help us apprehend this stylistic change from the musical aspect. In the verse chronicle the melody was subordinated to the words. Now it assumed a greater independence, in obedience to musical inspiration. The modes were slowly pervaded by major-minor tonality, making the melody smoother, more pleasing, and sometimes more sentimental. In place of a parlando rhythm or one made up of simple basic formulae, deliberately applied formations grew into independent shaping factors of music. Just as the speech-like music of the sixteenth century was adequate for poems mostly of an epic character, so now the lyrical character of literature was reflected in music unfolding melodically.

Within an overall character of change a certain amount of differentiation can be seen even on the basis of the few surviving examples. A more accessible, possibly more popular layer, sometimes going back to the Middle Ages, can be discerned. Good examples of this appear mainly in János Kájoni's manuscript collection.

Kájoni Codex in COHM, II, No. 169.

A nyúl a ve - te - mé - nyek kö - zött fü - lel,
A va - dá - szok pe - dig ke - re - sik széj-jel,

Bokros helyeken futkosnak, Te-li to-rok-kal ki-ált- nak, hu - lá - lá!

(The hare harks among the vegetables,
and the hunters are looking for it all round,
running about in the coppice and shouting at the top of their lungs, hulala!)

On the other hand, examples are also found–particularly in the Vietoris tablature book, notated by an anonymous musician around 1680–of a more sentimental, Baroque-like *bel canto* style, closer to art music:

Vietoris Tablature, No. 1 (Musicalia Danubiana 5).
Text on the basis of the Vásárhely Song Book.

Térj meg már búj-do-sá-sid - ból, És egy -

szer már sza-ba - dulj, Bú-val e - mész - tő-dött lel - kem...

(Return from your wanderings, and shake yourself free, my soul pining with grief...)

But a more graphic outline of the style is given by folk-music layers going back to the seventeenth century than by written sources. For here, instead of individual tunes, one is presented with melodic families which certainly have as their background common practice rather than individual taste. Outstanding in this folk-music repertoire is a rich family of melodies which exercised an influence for several decades. Their Phrygian melodies and fragmented yet clear form well characterize the whole period. Variants can be found both in vocal music (congregational hymns and lyrical songs) and instrumental dance music. Their appearance in contemporary song books supports their dating.

a.) Folk-music recording, Nagyszalonta, Bihar County. *See* Kodály, Z.: Folk-music of Hungary, 1971, No. 133.

b.) "Chorea", dance from the Kájoni Codex, quoted by Kodály, Z.: Folk-music of Hungary, Budapest, 1971, No. 137.

c.) Folk-music collection from Somogy County. Hungarian Academy of Sciences, Folk-music Archives.

d.) Folk-music recording from Verőce County. Hungarian Academy of Sciences, Folk-music Archives.

A word should be added about the social basis of this group of songs. People who wrote down the words (or tunes) include musicians interested in them, members of the nobility listing the songs they knew, notaries, teachers, army officers and students. A considerable part of the repertory was preserved in folk music. All of which seems to point to a Hungarian-speaking middle class of a fairly modest educational level originating and maintaining the body of songs, and who also were in contact both with the

Sert   a né - met - nek!

Hogy-ha   len -   ne ben-ne.

Hogy po-kol-ban   ne ki- ált-sak   vég-he- tet-len   jajt,   jajt.

*(Hey, let's go away from here, because here they'll beat us up,
let's not go away as long as they are fiddling. Bring wine for the Hungarian, brandy
for the Slovak, beer for the German!)*

*(Have a drink, now there's something in it, now you can do so,
you'd drink it, tippling dog, on a Friday, on a Saturday, without
minding, without minding, even out of the skin of a hairy dog, if
only there would be something left in it!).*

*(My poor self yearns for my Lord,
bending my remorseful heart to Him, Oh my God, how many are my sins,
show me the balm so that I should not cry in endless woe in hell!)*

upper strata of the peasantry and the lower strata of musicians in public service. The song repertory itself is "public poetry', which, in spite of its art music features, forms
common poetry in the manner of folk-music, being varied
and handed down from hand to hand or mouth to mouth.

Dance Music

The *Kájoni Codex* and the *Vietoris Tablature* are important sources in another respect as well. These collections are not groups of compositions, so much as miscellaneous favourite pieces of average musicians or amateurs. The *Vietoris Tablature,* for instance, contains a number of Hungarian and Slovak secular songs, church hymns, dances, trumpet duos and organ preludes, which, simple though they are, give a good picture of the average music of an age.

Dance pieces occupy much space in these manuscripts. They constitute a heterogeneous mass of material in their character, origin and treatment. Hungarian dances known as *Ungaresca* are found in sources abroad as early as in the sixteenth century, though it is hardly possible to see a clear musical difference between them and the *polonica,* the gipsy dance, the chorea or the allemande.

Instead we find a stylistic stratification ranging from unstylized stamping dances strung together from units of a few bars, possibly of a twin-bar structure:

"Roguish" dance from the Kájoni Codex.
In Szabolcsi, B.: Handbook of the History of Hungarian Music,
Collection of Examples, No. VI/3c.

Through more melodious dances in a fairly pliant rhythm, sometimes already influenced by the major-minor harmonic system, to real suite dances:

a.) "Hungarica" from the Vietoris Tablature Book, No. 101
(Musicalia Danubiana 5).

b.) Chorea from the Lőcse Tablature Book.
In Szabolcsi, B.: Handbook of the History of Hungarian Music,
Collection of Examples, VI/3y.

As can be seen, even the harmonization and the texture vary. Sometimes there is a primitive accompaniment, almost recalling folk-style (mainly in the *Kájoni Codex*, where our knowledge of the notator makes it clear that this texture is due not to his musical deficiency, but serves to depict a style), or just a sketch confined to a two-part texture which we may interpret as a melody and a figured bass (with some deficiencies, here due to the notator), as in the *Vietoris Tablature*). But we also find examples of an elaborate, fairly advanced musical fabric, not far removed from the keyboard technique of the Western European suite music of the day (the Sopron "Stark" virginal book, the Lőcse tablature).

These books give us an insight into the *Gebrauchsmusik* of the period, domestic music-making and the repertoire of semi-professionals and amateurs. (The Sopron virginal book, for example, was written for use by a middle-class family). And their pages also reflect the outlines of deeper dance-music traditions, even those of a folk character. It was these that held the promise of much that was to come in the following centuries.

5 The Baroque and Classical Periods

(18th Century)

Our orchestra used to be well provided for. However, during the last three years two of the musicians have died, and one has had to be dismissed due to his own fault, while another one is very old and can no longer perform his duties ... Two others do not wish to stay with the ensemble because of the duty of singing the office (plainsong). Our organist, who is well versed in his art, will remain here, as will another, who sings tenor and is a violinist. – This letter was written in 1742 by the canon responsible for the music at Pécs cathedral. Directed by his bishop, he began negotiations with his colleague at St Stephen's cathedral in Vienna about the reorganization of the orchestra. Their long correspondence at last bore fruit: Franz Anton Paumon, a member of the cathedral choir (himself a composer) undertook the post of choirmaster at Pécs and also to recruit further members and instruments for the orchestra, as well as to have scores copied, (although the letter of reply made it clear that the former composer and choirmaster Péter Pack, had assembled a large library of scores at Pécs). A long line of wagons set off from Vienna, and by 11 May, the musicians arrived in Pécs with their families, instruments and scores. On Trinity Sunday, Paumon, the *Maistro di Capell Musicae* made his debut with his new ensemble in the cathedral. Typical of the musicians making up the ensemble was the fact that bass was familiar with plainchant and played trumpet, first violin and French horn. The alto also knew plainsong, and played trumpet, trombone, cello and French horn. The first trumpet player also played trombone, cello, French horn and sang. Naturally two boys singing discantus were not absent from the ensemble.

In 1683, the Turks set out in full force to besiege Vienna. Extreme peril caused the armies of Western Europe to join forces at last to drive them back, and only now did it become clear how much strength the formidable enemy had lost. Within a few years they were driven out of the whole territory of Hungary (the liberation of Buda: 1686, the Peace of Karlóca /Sremski Karlovci/: 1699). Hungary, now liberated, attempted to ensure its independence and set out on the road towards a new life. But after the defeat of the wars of independence wage by Imre Thököly and Prince Ferenc Rákóczi II, the house of Habsburg consolidated its rule and the country sank into a semi-colonial state. Indeed, Joseph II (1780–1790) wanted to Germanize Hungary and assimilate it within his empire.

After the expulsion of the Turks and the sub-siding storms of the wars of freedom (1711), re-construction began in the country. Although Habsburg interests and the reinforced system of aristocratic large estates hamstrung any improvement in the economic situation, the system of political institutions only functioning properly at the level of county self-government, still, the rate of progress resulted in the resettlement of villages within some 20-30 years (for the most part by settlers from abroad: at this period the Hungarian-speaking population became a minority in its own country). There was a reconstruction of towns, the construction of hundreds of Baroque churches and palaces, public buildings, and manor houses, and the establishment of urban life, a characteristic folk culture was wrought out of a synthesis of old and new elements, and religious devotion gave rise to an abundance both on a higher level, and in more folk-oriented expression.

Aristocratic Residences

Despite the important achievements of the urban musical culture of the previous period, even in the field of music the effects of the previous 150 years could only be removed by a vigorous re-commencement. At the turn of the seventeenth and eighteenth centuries the impetus for this came from aristocratic and ecclesiastic patrons. In a number of aristocratic residences, the family, having moved back from Vienna and settled in Hungary, wished to underline their social and political standing not just with a Baroque palace and a luxurious way of life, but by patronizing music and literature. This aristocracy encountered in Vienna the musical formations, styles and repertoire whose introduction into Hungary now initiated a musical life throughout the country.

The Esterházy family boasted the greatest results in this field. Pál Esterházy (1635–1713), the son of a nobleman who had brought about the rapid rise of his family, was a military field officer, an imperial prince and the palatine of Hungary. A highly educated political thinker as well as a writer, poet and musician, the prince played the virginals, and in 1711 published his collection, *Harmonia Caelestis*, probably written between 1680 and 1700. This consisted of 55 pieces of church music, the simplest being short songs and duets accompanied by a string ensemble, or occasionally concertante solo instruments, while the more elaborate pieces have alternations of choir and solo voice, or an orchestral ritornello joining the vocal section. There are some lengthier aria-like pieces and one piece may be called a cantata in several sections. The majority are technically perfect, melodically attractive, mostly homophonic Baroque compositions or adaptations. (Some of the pieces are not original works but arrangements of hymns or other compositions, partly adapted to Esterházy's poems).

Esterházy, P.: Duet from Harmonia Caelestis, No. 24
(Musicalia Danubiana 10.)

(Jesus enters the garden and is betrayed by Judas. He is disdained and beaten by the ill-doers. They drag away my beloved one, my sweet one.)

The orchestra Pál Esterházy set up in his Kismarton castle matched in significance his fine publication. Consisting of some 10-12 members, as was customary at the time, it was gradually expanded by the prince's successors, so that by the time the family moved to their more sumptuous palace at Eszterháza (Fertőd) in the second half of the eighteenth century, it formed a large, established, 30-40 member ensemble of vocalists and virtuoso instrumentalists. They also had a theatre (opera) building of their own, which provided a unique opportunity in Central Europe for high-standard performances. From 1728, the ensemble was led for nearly forty years by Gregor Joseph Werner (1693–1766), a pupil of Fux. When Prince Miklós Esterházy (himself an accomplished instrumentalist) felt the late–Baroque style to be outdated, he engaged Joseph Haydn as vice *Kapellmeister*. From 1766, Haydn was the musical director of the orchestra, and many of his operas, symphonies and chamber works are linked to the Esterházy court. Though in 1790 the orchestra ceased to function for a short while and Haydn moved to Vienna, he maintained contact with the ensemble when it was reestablished and with Hungarian musical life throughout his life (as composer and conductor). Haydn's successor to the post of music director at Eszterháza was J.N. Hummel. Though the orchestra served mainly to bring the best music of the day, at the highest level, to the residents at Eszterháza (Fertőd), its members occasionally also made guest appearances in neighbouring towns and cities (Sopron, Pozsony /Bratislava/), contributing greatly to making this region of two or three counties by the turn of the century be in the country's front-rank with their outstanding and exemplary musical achievements.

. None of the other aristocratic residences in the country reached, at least on a lasting footing, the level of the musical life in the Esterházy residence. But its example was followed by others, each contributing to the fact that by the second half of the century orchestras of varying sizes and chamber ensembles appeared in many parts of the country. In Nagyvárad (Oradea), for instance, there was a musical centre with high standards for some time in the household of Bishop Ádám Patachich, the musicians performing operas and oratorios on a regular basis. Michael Haydn, and later Dittersdorf were active there for some years as conductors and composers. The 8 to 10 musicians engaged by the Tata branch of the Esterházy family were also sufficient, as the surviving music library shows, for the performance of church and chamber music by leading and minor classical composers. The second half of the century saw various ensembles of repute in aristocratic houses in Pozsony (Bratislava), some of which undertook the performance of operas.

⸗ But even in cases when only one or two domestic musicians could be employed, this already increased the demand for music in Hungarian society. György Festetics, an enlightened aristocrat, set up a music school beside his Keszthely family seat and acquired a large collection of scores. Data concerning the musicians of the Végh family of Vereb and their surviving music library offer a typical example of a modest but continuous musical life. The first violinist of the Vereb ensemble, István Franz, for instance, was the son of a musician at Kismarton (Eisenstadt), he himself came to Vereb from the Pozsony (Bratislava) family of the Batthyánys, later touring Hungarian towns and cities giving concerts, and finally becoming director of the court theatre in Vienna. The Brunswick family were also famous for their love of music, they had a piano teacher, Ferenc Kleinheinz, Count Ferenc played the cello and was a friend of Beethoven, being his host on several occasions at Martonvásár. Beethoven dedicated the Appassionata Sonata to him. Another member of Beethoven's circle of friends was Miklós Zmeskall, a nobleman from Upper Hungary, who was an official at the chancellery and also active as a cellist and a composer.

It should be kept in mind that most of these families also maintained town houses (in Vienna, Pozsony /Bratislava/, and later in Pest or Buda) besides their residences on their estates, and the ensembles they engaged there had a marked influence on fairly wide circles of society.

Church Orchestras

The second sphere of reconstruction of musical life also belonged to the type that served the *internal* musical needs of institutions, though it still stood in closer proximity to society than the first. After the expulsion of the Turks, the Catholic bishops returned to their seats, rebuilding their cathedrals in Baroque style and organizing the musical life along Western lines. The few episcopal sees that had not been occupied by the Turks, thus continuing to function without a break, reorganized their musical life in the same spirit early in the eighteenth century. These attempts were evident already early in the century but their position became firmly established only by the mid-century. This orchestral style was exemplified in Pécs, Győr, Veszprém, Székesfehérvár and Szombathely, whose orchestras were founded in the second half of the century, and, a little later, in Eger.

The ensembles usually consisted of 2-4 violinists, 2-3 viola-players, 2-4 woodwind players, 2-3 male vocalists and 4-5 boy choristers. Depending on the works performed, the musicians played several instruments, and also took part in singing figural music, and the obligatory plainsong. The cathedral divine services had set order: the public mass with Hungarian congregational hymns was led by the organist, the weekday masses and office usually had Gregorian chant in the new Roman version, but on special occasions there were polyphonic pieces as well (e.g. the Rorate introit at morning masses during Advent). On Sundays and feast days high mass and vespers were polyphonic, with Gregorian additions.

The repertoire, at least in the second half of the century, can be reconstructed from the manuscript parts of several hundred in places several thousand works extant in music libraries. The majority are by Caldara, Albrechtsberger,

Georg Reutter, Michael Haydn, and a whole range of Southern German, Austrian and Italian minor composers. Masses by Haydn and Mozart, and works by local or Hungarian composers can also be found. As regards musical genres, orchestral masses, vespers, magnificats, litanies and antiphons of the Blessed Virgin predominate, but chamber music and orchestral parts for symphonies also indicate that the musicians were employed outside the church as well. The manuscripts in many cases also include the dates of performances, which helps us draw up an even clearer picture of actual practice.

The number of musicians listed were often not sufficient for the works to be performed. Sporadic data suggests that sometimes the piece concerned was re-orchestrated, but in most cases the ensemble itself was expanded by musicians from other churches in the town, by military musicians, instrumentalists summoned from neighbouring towns, or students studying music. This also reveals to us that a new, civic musicians confratarnity was slowly growing up around the cathedral musicians.

In some towns the musical ensembles of large parish churches functioned on similar lines using a similar repertoire, but possibly with smaller numbers of musicians. Their work in this case was helped by established traditions. The patron of the municipal church was the town itself, making the occasional participation of tower musicians (or *waits*) in the church orchestra a natural course. Usually there were links between the school and the church choir as well, which meant that there was no need to engage boys singing discantus since the leader of the choir (*regens chori*) also taught in the school and could select the boys from there. The best examples of this type of municipal ensemble were those of the Pest parish church set up in the 1720s, and the Sopron parish church, which was in rivalry with the Lutherans.

The calendar records and score libraries of some of the Catholic grammar schools (belonging to the Piarists and the Jesuits) indicate a highly developed musical life. Besides attending to music in the church, musicians there participated in school festivals, doctoral disputations and graduations, and also in the interludes of school plays, which were sometimes almost operas (of these unfortunately only description survived, without the music).

The schools and churches in the Lutheran towns worked upon similar lines building upon seventeenth century foundations. The collection of scores at Sopron provides an imposing picture of this, with a large number of cantatas alongside the traditional genres, from the mid-eighteenth century onwards (e.g. nearly 100 works by Cristoph Stolzenberg of Regensburg). True, this gradually came to be an exception, as the restrictions imposed on Lutherans slowly eroded the practice of high-standard art-music in most of their churches, the lead being taken by chorales translated from German.

Congregational hymns sung in Hungarian also played a leading role in most of the Catholic churches. Aside from the churches discussed already, encounter with the latest music–at varying levels–was only possible in a few monasteries (for instance at Pannonhalma) or in the town churches of religious orders. These decades saw the emergence of a strange, heterogeneous kind of church music among the Franciscans and the Paulites (a Hungarian order founded in 1263). Its starting point was a simplified Gregorian chant compressed into strict measures, and accompanied by figured bass. This gradually gave place to compositions incorporating Gregorian-like, and finally Baroque-like motifs. The style not only shows what meagre resources these communities had at their disposal but also threw light on an opposite path: instead of selecting from modern music the things that fitted the simpler environment, it set out from early monophony and strove upwards by adding to it elements taken from art music.

Missa tubicinalis from the Franciscan Manuscript of Veszprém.
Issued by Szigeti, K. in Magyar Zene (Hungarian Music), 1978,
pp. 282-97.

(Lord, have mercy upon us...)

Changes in the 18th Century

So far we have presented this century as a whole. In fact, however, its most important occurrence lay precisely in a change, a shift.

The majority of both the residential and cathedral orchestras came into being at the request of an aristocrat or a bishop,who from the outset defined the orchestra's make-up, repertory and style But where did the people, instruments and scores necessary for this come from? At their time of origin, these ensembles functioned as islands within society not only because they served only an internal musical life of a residence or a cathedral, but also because they consisted of musicians almost all of whom had come from abroad. Sometimes a whole orchestra arrived in one block: leaders and players, complete with their families, belongings, instruments and scores. Even if they were engaged singly–either now or later–nonetheless they bore German-Austrian or Bohemian names. Such comings and goings went on throughout the century: players could be exchanged, change places, with new ones arriving from abroad. The leading orchestra–like the one at Eszterháza–always gave preference to noted foreigners.

A knowledge of the preceding centuries, of course, makes this practice understandable. One of the processes which marks out the eighteenth century is precisely the development of a Hungarian musical confraternity. This took place in two forms: one, the settlement of foreign musicians, establishing families and becoming incorporated into the town's society, bringing up children who followed in the occupation of their fathers. The other path led via the appearance of local musicians trained for the profession: discanting boys, the children of urban citizens and music students in grammar schools, who choose the musical profession.

The cathedral musicians also emerged from out of their isolation. They began to make guest appearances in other churches, to perform in town festivals, parades and receptions, often being engaged even as entertainment musicians. A decisive step was the opening of music schools, as they established direct musical contact with ordinary citizens, and trained a young generation which might opt for a musical career or become amateur musicians. A music school was set up in Buda in 1727, and by the end of the century "in all the better households there was a piano". By the end of the eighteenth century, the music school of Pécs had 18 instrumental students, their number growing to 55 by 1809 (37 children coming from middle-class families). A music loving German traveller who visited Pécs in 1793 found Mozart and Pleyel sonatas and variations on the music stand of a burgher family, and another traveller reports of intensive domestic music-making going on in Pest.

- By the second half of the century the same church musicians became the chief organizers and performers of public concerts, called "academies". These were no longer exclusive musical evening in manor houses or episcopal palaces, nor occasions for church devotion where music played a subsidiary role. City dwellers, reared on music they had encountered in the church, in the streets and at balls, or had learnt in the music schools, gathered now together, and indeed payed to listen to programmes which at first were fairly miscellaneous (Symphonies, concerto movements, chamber and solo pieces, four-hand music and duets, performed by amateurs and professionals, all offered in one and the same programme.)

- This already touches on the third component of the process of change. The music of the town concentrated around several centres, slowly overstepping feudal bounds, and producing new aspects in the relationship of the middle-class to music. The most important feature was the presence of a learned professional musicians whom the citizen encountered in various functions. Military bands, miners' ensembles and gipsy bands also appeared and by the second half of the century a growing number of theatrical companies were playing musical works for the stage. The continuity of musical life was now not only–and not principally–ensured by the church and aristocratic patrons who realized its significance, but to a growing extent by citizens ready to spend money on it.

- The first results of this process were felt in Pozsony (Bratislava), the capital of Hungary at the time. This is hardly surprising as the citizens there had become accustomed to high-level church music over the centuries, in both Catholic and Lutheran churches. Ensembles were active in princely houses, and in the city's theatre travelling companies followed one upon another. The musical centres were in this area scarcely 20-30 kilometres distance from one another, and musicians could be called in from abroad to good positions, all of which created a healthy mobility among the musicians. By the end of the century for someone to earn his living by teaching music entailed no real risk. After the 1780s, there were always at least 3-4 good composer/choirmasters and 20-30 instrumental musicians active in the city. The nearness of Vienna also helped, both by ensuring guest performances and the quick transmission of new works. Mozart's operas and the works of Haydn and Beethoven were heard in Pozsony (Bratislava) sometimes only one or two years after their composition.

This was true not only of Pozsony. Though the privileged position of Pozsony enabled it to meet faster and at a higher level a demand generally felt by that time, even so Pest, Buda (Haydn and Beethoven concerts), Győr, Szeben (Sibin) (opera performances) and Kolozsvár (where debate surrounding Beethoven's music degenerated into a free-for-all early in the nineteenth century), Pécs, Sopron, and a few other towns proceeded essentially along the same path.

Composers

Like Werner, Haydn and later Hummel at Eszterháza (Fertőd), other orchestras were also led by *Kapellmeisters* (musical directors) who, to the best of their gifts, enriched the repertoires of their ensembles with their own works. By the end of the century, there is evidence of a stream of Hungarian composition which went beyond provincial limitations.

The music in the score collections of the first half of the century offers little insight into the repertoire and its composers' works, at least until a thorough study throws light on the provenance of the many hundreds of anonymous works. Nor is it easy to draw a picture of the composers of the classical period, as a great many of their works have been lost, and only a few of the surviving ones have been transcribed into score from the original parts.

Benedek Istvánffy (1733–1776), from a Hungarian gentry family, was the son of a professional musician who worked at Pannonhalma, Veszprém and Bakonybél, and who was the first teacher of his son. After his student years in Sopron, Benedek became domestic organist to the Széchényi family, later being engaged as conductor of the cathedral orchestra at Győr, which had a distinguished history. Before his early death he did much to raise the standards of the orchestra and enrich its repertoire with his own works and by copying out dozens of works for them. His two surviving orchestral masses and several minor church works reveal him to be an inventive early-classical composer with a good sense of form and an engaging musical personality.

Istvánffy, Benedek: Duetto, bars 7-14
(Musicalia Danubiana 3, p. 133)

(O Jesus, my beloved one, you were born for me,
you glorious Child, you shall be our redeemer...)

(Church compositions by two other members of the Győr ensemble, the horn-player Ignác Kunáth and the singer Flórián Jazitsek also survived.)

The musical director of the Pest city church was Joseph Bengraf (1745–1791), who settled there from Germany. Besides some large church works, he wrote string quarters in the style of the early Haydn quartets, piano pieces, music for town festivities, and Hungarian style dance compositions. Valentin Deppisch (1746–1782), a contemporary of Bengraf, was the musical director at Pécs cathedral, his pleasant-sounding, well shaped masses, a requiem and

several church works, arias and symphonies bespeak his
proficiency in classical technique. His predecessors at Pécs
were composers of a similar style (Franz Antol Paumon,
György Svoboda, Miklós Strobach), while his successor,
Ferenc Novotni, a pupil of Kotzeluch in Vienna, was a
well-known composer by the time he settled in Pécs in
1782. Surviving copies in music collections in Sopron,
Győr, Veszprém and Vienna show that his church works
were widely circulated.

Of the composers active in princely residences, an
example is Péter Stärk, who served with the Festetics family at Keszthely. Franz Krommer (Kramář), who from
1818 gained renown as a court composer at Vienna, was
earliers for some time the conductor of the count's orchestra at Simontornya, later working at Pécs cathedral.

Mention must be made of a few of the many composers
in Pozsony (Bratislava) late in the eighteenth century:
Anton Zimmermann (1741?–1781) was conductor of the
Batthyány orchestra, composing symphonies and chamber
music notable for both quality and quantity (a sextet, 12
string quintets, 12 flute quintets, a violin sonata) as well
as concertos and masses. One of his melodramas was performed in Vienna. Franz Rigler (?–1797) was a music
teacher (with J.N.Hummel as one of his pupils) and also
gave concerts. Apart from his piano pieces, he made his
name with a piano and music-theory tutor printed in Vienna and Pest. Henrik Klein (1756–1832), a music teacher
in the municipal school (one of his pupils was Ferenc
Erkel), and a contributor to the Leipzig *Allgemeine Musi-
kalische Zeitung*, composed piano fantasias, cantatas and
masses. The theatre chorus master Franz Tost (*c.* 1754–
1829) wrote chamber-music works, stage works and a cantata with Hungarian words.

Two composers deserve more detailed attention: the
Bohemian-born Georg Druschetzky (1745–1819) who

worked at Pozsony in the 1790s, and then, for twenty years played in the Pest orchestra of the Palatine Joseph, and János Fusz (1777–1819), a musician born in Hungary of German stock, but educated in Hungary. Druschetzky's huge oeuvre as a composer has remained virtually unpublished. About 100 wind chamber pieces, brass and timpani concertos, operas, church works, symphonies and string quartets bear witness to his fertility, technical assurance, and above all an imagination excelling in virtuoso instrumental treatment.

Druschetzky, G.: Partita in E♭, fourth movement
(Musicalia Danubiana 4, p. 88)

Fusz for a few years worked for the Végh family, later living and working alternately in Pozsony (Bratislava), Vienna and Pest. He was a musician on a grand scale, already tending towards Romanticism (his output includes melodramas, operas, a pantomime, church music, piano sonatas and chamber music.) Beethoven praised his vocal pieces. Nearly sixty of Fusz's works appeared in print, a great part of the manuscript copies now being in Vienna, while a few are preserved in Hungarian score collections.

Fusz, J.: Funeral march on the death of Albrechtsberger.
Contemporaneous print, Vienna, Cappi, bars 15-22.

Moderato con afflizione

The majority of these composers (together with their colleagues not listed here) undoubtedly reached the standard of contemporary Austrian, Bohemian and German minor masters. More cannot be said about their personalities until their works are raised from almost total oblivion in the form of score editions and concert performances.

Students' Songs

Knowing what went before, the situation outlined above would be satisfactory if one were able to project it over Hungary as a whole. In fact, however, the picture is valid for only a narrow area both geographically and socially. Contrary to the promising endeavours of a few towns in Transdanubia, Upper Hungary and Transylvania, huge territories remained untouched by a contemporary musical practice and culture. This in turn prevented the development of a mobile number of professional musicians who could span the country as a whole, as well as of the channels to receive them.

This was due to the fact that in the education of the gentry and the intelligentsia, the strata which otherwise would have been principally receptive to higher musical cultivation, music lagged disproportionately behind humanistic learning. The medieval ideal linking musical and literary cultivation was a thing of the past. Most of this middle class considered a musical profession alien to their traditions, and virtually unworthy of them. Schools and colleges–particularly the Calvinist ones–which educated the lower intellectual classes who fulfilled the role of the bourgeoisie, were expressly hostile to music of a high standard.

The Calvinist Church ousted art music and instruments from the church on principle. In the seventeenth and eighteenth centuries prohibitive measures were taken by school organizers against instrumental studies and even spontaneous music-making. And since the regular musical practice of the church was lacking in providing the elevating experience of higher music, puritan views lumped together dallying musical revelries with decent chamber music.

And this did not remain an intramural matter of schools. In Calvinist towns the church, the school and the municipal leadership created an indivisible and unifrom public climate. The practice of legates (older students operating in a pastoral and teaching capacity in the neighbouring villages) extended these norms to villages as well. And finally, most college graduates left the inspiring urban atmosphere and withdrew to their country estates, where they conserved, as it were, their school experiences. Socially linked by a common realm of experiences and scale of values, influential both politically and intellectually and spread over the whole country they represented a fairly unifrom "second line" behind the "first line" of the aristocracy and church dignitaries.

The musical material of a Calvinist college was the monophonic congregational song, primarily the Geneva psalms in Hungarian translation. These were complemented by funeral songs (since singing at funerals was a duty and a source of income for college students.)

But of course, students in the long run cannot exist without some form of secular music. This stock of songs might at first have consisted of the lyrical songs inherited from the seventeenth century, but the eighteenth century brought a change in this respect. A picture of the songs of the college students can easily be found, as from the mid-eighteenth century onwards several hundreds have survived in many collections in a primitive musical notation.

Althoug stylistically the material is not homogeneous, there are still a few common features. Melodically, they show the use of simplified figures of triads, frequent melodic turns springing from broken chords, and sequences of seconds or thirds. There are occasional traces of the seventeenth century Phrygian song, but the majority of the pieces are in major keys. Given their simple metrical and rhythmic formulae and mostly simple formal schemes, one can only characterize them by saying that they comprise a quite banal repertoire of tunes. This would not have mattered if they had not constituted practically the sole musical nourishment of the students and the middle classes which came from them. That the repertoire of these collections was not a passing feature of their student years, but a determining factor in their musical horizons for life is well reflected in the song collection of a nobleman from early in the nineteenth century, Ádám Pálóczi Horváth's *Ötödfélszász Énekek* (Four and a Half Hundred Songs). Ranging from patriotic songs to lewd students' songs, they present a good overall picture of the music stored away in the memory of a learned man in his mature years.

The material of these songs can be stratified historically and stylistically. Some are fairly noble melodies, with folksong reflexes stretching back to the seventeenth century:

Zemplény Manuscript, in Szabolcsi, B.: Handbook of the History of Hungarian Music, Collection of Examples, No. VIII/2b.

Hej, Rá-kó-czi, Ber-csé-nyi, ma-gyar vi- té - zek ne- mes ve - zé - ri!

Ho-vá let - tek, ho- vá men-tek vá - lo - ga - tott vi - té - zi?

(Hey, Rákóczi, Bercsényi, gallant leaders of Hungarian warriors!
Where did the select champions go, where did they disappear to?)

Others are simple forms compiled from musical stereotypes in the major, with sequential melodic contours:

Patak Collection of Melodies,
in Bartha, D.: Eighteenth Century Hungarian Melodies, No. 40.

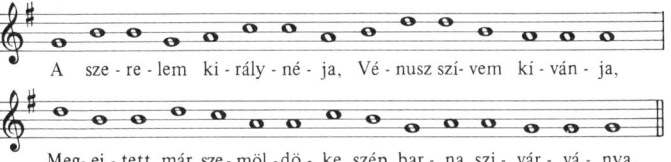

A sze - re - lem ki - rály - né - ja, Vé - nusz szí- vem ki - ván - ja,

Meg- ej - tett már sze- möl - dö - ke szép bar - na szi - vár - vá - nya.

(The queen of love, Venus, my heart's desire,
I have been captured by the fine brown rainbow of her brow.)

Some melodies show the influence of German art music:

István Tóth's manuscript.
In Bartha, D.: Eighteenth Century Hungarian Melodies, No. 106.

Szép haj - nal, e - meld fel föl - dünk fe - lett,

(etc.)

az e - gek a - latt tün - dök - lő szent fák - lyá - dat! . . .

(Fair dawn, lift your holy torch, which shines over the earth and under the sky...)

Some are fashionable tunes with an AABA (ABBC) form which consist of more than one clearcut lines and are enlivened by a fragmented middle section:

Patak Collection of Melodies,
in Bartha, D.: Eighteenth Century Hungarian Melodies, No. 59.

Im-már Vé-nusz el - vet-te   a szép al - mát, mint ju-tal - mát
Melyért vi- dám szí- ve ö - rül,   al-má - já - ért, pál-má-já - ért,

ke - be- lé - be   rej -tet - te.   Táncra va-gyon vé - ná- ja,
mél-tó ö - röm - be me -rül.   Gyönggyel nyílik a   szá-ja,

Si - et e - lé   Cziprus fe - lé,   mert ott va - gyon   ha- zá - ja.

*(Venus has already taken the fine apple as her prize
and hidden it in her breast. Her gay heart rejoices over this,
she is lost in just delight over her apple, over her palm.
She is in the mood to dance, her lips part with pearls,
she hurries to Cyprus, for there is her homeland.)*

And there are more complex "Rococo" melodies fashioned from a palyful string of tiny motifs:

Zemplény Manuscript,
in Bartha, D.: Eighteenth Century Hungarian Melodies, No. 22.

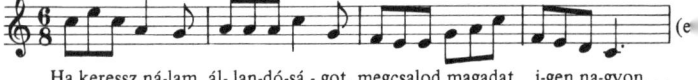

Ha keressz ná-lam ál- lan-dó-sá - got, megcsalod magadat   i-gen na-gyon. . .

(If you look for constancy in me, you shall greatly disappoint yourself...)

Thus there was some sort of development, but it is quite another matter whether this represented any gain aesthetically. The melodies sound stereotyped, the easier sound pampering taste and turning it towards the easy and alluring. The majority of the songs indeed seem musically to radiate a kind of flippancy. At the same time they also indicate a change in the role music way playing. Already in the texts there begins to appear a heterogeneous, almost incoherent juxtaposition, which in all probability marks a blurring of genres and through it a weakening of sense of social function. In other words, the songs are just songs, ditties, a fill up for occasions to sing. It took a lot to arrest this process of decline in seriousness.

"Singing in Harmony"

The barriers that were raised in this area are well reflected in the fate of an attempt by György Maróthi (1715–1744). A teacher at the Calvinist college in Debrecen, Maróthi wanted to put to good use his experiences gained during a study tour in Switzerland by introducing three innovations in his school in the 1740s:

1. The introduction of the three-part song he discovered in Switzerland, a form of light triadic music with pietistic words which acted as a kind of unofficial musical pastime intended as a *collegium musicum* (private gatherings). He translated a selection of the pieces he had brought back home and had them printed, but was not granted permission to use them.

2. The introducing of the teaching of music reading and sight-singing in church. But a clash between the "correct" melodies and the accustomed variants led to objections and an outcry, and the city authorities banned the use of written music.

3. The introduction with a small group of students of "chordal singing". He adapted to Hungarian words the four-part textures of Goudimel's psalms he had brought back from Switzerland, and had them published in the hope that this small group would cause the spread of polyphonic singing in the school as a whole, the school then doing in the neighbouring villages.

Although his efforts caused no real breakthrough for polyphonic music, the students became fond of "singing in harmony", and when not applying it to psalms, they readily sang their favourite students' songs with home-made, clumsy part-writing progressing in large blocks of triads and crammed with consecutives.

Patak Collection of Melodies, in Szabolcsi, B.: Handbook of the History of Hungarian Music, Collection of Examples, No. IX/2e.

Nem-ze- te - met si- ra - tom, nagy e - gek-nek e - rős u - ra, tartsd meg . . .

(I bewail for my nation, powerful Lord of heaven, save it...)

The popularity of this style is borne out by recordings in students' collections (with peculiar "scores" containing no rhythm in indications, and using sometimes 8-10 lines on a stave, and various geometrical figures indicating the parts), and also by the fact that name-day greeting songs sung in such primitive polyphony were still found and recorded in Calvinist villages in the twentieth century.

When one remembers that about 200 kilometres away from these schools urban audiences listened to Haydn's music, while there a battle had to be fought (and unsuccessfully) for the introduction of a most simple chordal technique, which was 200 years out of date, then the picture is quite depressing. There the "German" trend was not accompanied by an adequate social background. Here Maróthi deserves the credit for wanting to involve his own, Hungarian students instead of hiring foreign musicians to sing his psalm harmonies.

This is the point where one can clearly see the anomaly Kodály diagnosed 150 years later when he said that educated people were not Hungarian enough and the Hungarians were not educated enough. What was of a higher quality musically had a much too narrow social foundation in Hungary, and what the broader middle classes cultivated was musically of little worth and unsuitable for development. While down below (at the "third level") folk music lived on, preserving its ancient beauties, and being influenced here and there by the newer influences.

The Origin of the *Verbunkos* Style

The only field where a contact between high music and widely popular music seemed possible was Hungarian dance music of the late eighteenth century.

The Hungarian-style pieces in the dance-music collections of the first half of the century, entitled *ungaresca*, and *saltus hungaricus*, still maintained the traditional style of the previous century, or perhaps centuries.

"Saltus hungaricus" from the Zsuzsa Lányi Manuscript, in Kodály, Z.: Retrospection II, pp. 275-76.

These *hungaricus* (Hungarian) dances figure in musical note-books of the period among mixed European surroundings (drawn from nay different fields), including minuets, steiers /*Landlers*/ and short pieces by Telemann, Graun, Vivaldi, Bach and Locatelli sonatas, fugues and variations, etc.). They are in books and noted down for private use, for domestic piano playing, in which the amateur musician put down everything he found to his liking. Such collections include the Apponyi manuscript, the manuscript of Zsuzsanna Lányi, and the collections of László Székely, Tádé Bodnár, etc. These sources in fact also show one of the routes taken by the spread of instrumental musical culture, namely the expansion of the musical horizons of amateurs.

Slowly there began in the Hungarian dances a new tone, a new repertoire of melodies, and a new manner of ornamentation. Instrumental adaptations of pieces of seventeenth century vocal music showed a melodic style that differed from old Hungarian dance music and its European environment. The augmentation and   of the swineherd's dance:

and/or its instrumental embellishment brought about a musical sentence form of 16 bars (two periods). The effect of this style was to spread the Dorian, Aeolian and finally minor tonalities, to the detriment of the pentachordal structure of the older dance music.

The style assumed its true characteristics though rhythmic patterns and ornamentation. Various, markedly articulated dottings (e.g. ♫♫), syncopation, strings of triplets and suspensions:

and typical cadential formulae:

make up a clearly identifiable "vocabulary" recognizable in the smallest elements of the pieces, and so are continually in evidence as indications of identity.

Dances of Galánta–Ausgesuchte ungarische Nationaltänze - 3,
see Musicalia Danubiana 7, p. 182.

This transformation had to stem from "below", among semi-professional folk instrumentalists and small ensembles providing dance music, partly the gipsy bands which grew up precisely at this time. By the turn of the century the style must have become widely familiar, as from the 1760s and '70s onwards it can be detected in the works of Austrian composers, who used it as *couleur locale* (Dittersdorf, Haydn: Piano Concerto in D major, Mozart: Violin Concerto in A major, Beethoven: Third Symphony, Diabelli: Hungarian Dances).

Meanwhile the Hungarian dance itself came gradually to contain elements of contemporary art music. It adapted itself to classical functional harmony, which extended its influence to the melody line. The 16-bar unit began to shape itself along the lines of classical binary form, even being coupled with a trio. The regular make-up of the ensemble was derived from that of the classical small orchestra (2 violins, viola, bass, clarinet and a cimbalom in place of the continuo). This amalgamation of a Hungarian tradition with art-music elements resulted, by about the 1770s, in a style which is usually called *verbunkos* (military recruiting dance).

And if the great figures in Vienna paid heed to it, then composers in Hungary were even more thoroughly aware of it. There was no church, stage or town composers during these decades, including those who were German or Czech-speaking who, whether from attraction to it or as the expression of "Hungarian" national feeling, did not compose a set or even sets of six or twelve Hungarian dances (Bengraf, Zimmermann, Rigler, Druschetzky, Klein, Tost, Vanhal, Krommer, etc.). These sets of dances for piano or small orchestra, either arrangements or character pieces in their own right, always took a middle course between the exact reproduction of the character of the original utility music and a compositional attitude employing the norms and technique of art music. The mutual interaction between art music and everyday practice (or indeed popular) music that prevailed from the inception of the style, formed the formulation the bold hopes for *verbunkos* cherished in the nineteenth century.

Rigler, Franz Paul: 12 ungarische Tänze, No. 9
Musicalia Danubiana 7, p. 106.

It took a non-musical factor to change the vogue for
down-to-earth late-eighteenth century Hungarian
"dances", either in its popular or its elaborated forms into
a veritable apotheosis of *verbunkos*. This factor was the
national movement that raised this music from a purely
colouristic role in the hope of making it the foundation of
a Hungarian art music that had never existed before.

6 The Romantic Period
(19th Century)

Extracts from letters written by Franz Liszt in 1839: "Arrived in Pozsony (Bratislava) at five o'clock in the morning. At noon today: my first concert. Yesterday supper with Count Batthyány (the present leader of the opposition in Hungary), visit to Széchenyi, who was perfectly kind to me.–My concert has just ended. Inexpressible enthusiasm ... Since at the end there was no end of applause, I played another Hungarian melody, by the way, I have written two more as well."

"The applause redoubled, and finally, when I started with the first chords of the Rákóczi March (a very popular tune in Hungary which I have now arranged after my own manner), the whole hall echoed with a single short 'Éljen! Éljen! (Vivat!)."

"We started out for Pest, where we arrived without any accident about four o'clock the day before yesterday ... About five thirty, I suddenly heard a wonderful sound of men's voices, they opened my door: about sixty people were gathered together in the next room, singing a quartet with chorus ... These sounds, this gathering of unknown friends, this celebration made a profound impression on me. Hardly was the quartet over when a huge military band (of some fifty to sixty musicians) assembled in the court-yard, and broke forcefully into a Hungarian tune which they attributed to me ... The performance was perfect, the intention most kind."

"Festetics in his hand, has a splendid sword, studded with turquoises, rubies, etc. He makes a short address in Hungarian before the whole audience, which applauds frantically, then he girds me with the sword in the name of the Nation.

"Last Wednesday, the day after the benefit concert I gave for the poor in Sopron, I made a pilgrimage to Doborján (Raiding). I recognized every village, every tower, the cart-tracks and even some of the houses along my road. I am at a loss to understand this persistence of childhood memories ... Some two miles from Doborján (Raiding), about twenty peasants, dressed in their finery, came to meet me on horse-back and accompanied me to the magistrate's house. The whole village (about a thousand people) were gathered there. The children–boys and girls–curtseyed to me. It took all my efforts to persuade them to stand up. A few peasants came to kiss my hand, but most of them remained at a respectful distance. The priest who came to meet me, took me to my family's house..."

The death in 1790 of Joseph II, Emperor of Austria and uncrowned King of Hungary, was followed by vehement reaction against his Germanizing policies despite their well-intentioned civilized aims. The movement was joined–naturally with varying interests–by the whole political life of Hungary, and broadened into a reform period lasting for several decades. It brought to the forefront the question of acting as a nation, the development of the country's economy and of proper institutions and culture, and the gradual cutting down of feudal privileges and boundaries. The Reform Period, and its leading figure Count István Széchenyi (1790–1861), the broad-visioned politician known as "the greatest Hungarian", gave rise to Hungary's most idealistic and at the same time realistic intellectual efforts, not only awakening the nation, but also acting as the source of its coming to maturity. At the same time, a grave mistake was committed (later proved to be tragic) not to realize that, in answer to the expansion of the German language (and annulling the centuries-long official use of Latin) making Hungarian the official language in a multi-national country, without modern provisions for relations with ethnic minorities, would lead to growing conflicts.

At first it seemed that, thanks to lengthy agreements and supported by the 1848 revolutions in Vienna and Pest, the reform movement would achieve considerable results without breaking with the House of Habsburg. But in the summer of 1848, the sudden hardening of Vienna's policy sparked off an armed confrontation. Faced with the Hungarian successes of the spring of 1849, the Vienna government called in Russian troops to assist, and by the end of the summer they had crushed the War of Independence. This was followed by years of drastic repression bringing with it the danger of total assimilation. Domestic and foreign political developments, however, forced Vienna to renegotiate. The Austro-Hungarian monarchy was brought forth by the *Ausgleich*, the Compromise with the Habsburgs, in 1867, enabled the setting up of an independent Hungarian government, except in foreign and military affairs and finance.

The four peaceful decades that followed 1867 brought rapid economic and social development to the country. This period saw spectacular results: the advance of capitalism, the construction of factories and railways, the unification and rapid growth of Buda and Pest, the gradual decrease in internal differences between the various regions of the country (hand in hand with growing differences between the new capital of Budapest and the provinces) and, after the ending of feudal land conditions, the emergence of an articulated class of peasantry, a modest working class and a wider layer of merchants, small industrialists and intellectuals. And all this, indirectly, also effected the musical scene.

Although with this "Compromise" went other compromises which caused the penalty Hungary, after entering the First World War on the side of Austria, had to pay in 1918: the loss of her thousand-year state unity.

The New Role of *Verbunkos*

The *verbunkos* style having reached the peak of its development, was just the music the burning national movement was crying out for in the early nineteenth century. Its pronounced eternal formulae were easily recognized, and people saw in them the "ancient" expression of Hungarian taste. (At the time it did not occur to anyone that the style had a mere 100 year of history, and not millennia). Gipsy musicians, particularly the legendary János Bihari, proved to be expert interpreters of the music, capable of forwarding its message with great instrumental virtuosity and sweeping fire. At the same time such music was inseparable from the romantic national dances embarking on their triumphal progress at this time, ranking as the principal expression of the Hungarian spirit for a generation who scorned to ape foreign ways.

The motto of the Reform Age was not just the "nation", but "progress" as well. Musically this appeared as a demand to develop an independent Hungarian art, music and to establish Hungarian opera and Hungarian symphonies. The decades-old interest of educate musicians in Hungarian dances prepared the way for a programme whereby the use of the national idiom–*verbunkos*–was to create a victorious Hungarian art music.

Looking back from the twentieth century, it is easy to see the weaknesses in such a project. Although the specific idiom of *verbunkos* was in keeping with Romanticism's attraction to unusual colour, it could still be best harmonized basically with the Classical musical idiom. Its narrow harmonic vocabulary and the formal and rhythmic framework inseparable from a structure of 8-bar periods were in complete contrast with nineteenth century endeavours: the breaking up of dividing lines between keys, and the conquest of open, large developing forms. It needed an utterly different approach and a genius to align these two kinds of musical mentality.

- The *verbunkos* style appeared in the music of the first half of the nineteenth century in four forms:

1. Its original form, or simply stylized by virtuoso performers, was a musical feature, or rather an admired attraction, at celebrations, and political or social get-togethers of the nobility. The stars of this manner of performance were János Bihari (1764–1827), János Lavotta (1764–1820), and later the musically trained Márk Rózsavölgyi (1789?–1848) who aimed at more polished examples.

2. The second form was found in the instrumental "arrangements" of Hungarian dance music. This differed in principle from the late eighteenth century arrangements by educated musicians inasmuch as the purely musical purpose was now joined by a desire to preserve and spread national values in a decent manner. At its lowest level, it appeared in the many collections made by mediocre musicians, in which the original musical form is reproduced with a fair accuracy (e.g. the volumes by the Pest music teacher Ágoston Mohaupt, the *Hungarian Songs from Veszprém County* containing 136 pieces, published by Ignác Ruzitska, etc.). The next level consisted of dances similar in genre, composed more or less independently (e.g. those by the church musician György Arnold of Szabadka, the composer András Bartay of Pest, etc.). The highest level of this form of *verbunkos* is represented by Franz Liszt's Hungarian fantasias.

3. The third form consists of compositions that employ the idiom of *verbunkos* in art-music forms. as an insertion.

Here, too, there are various grades. The *verbunkos* song (wether intended for independent performance, domestic music-making or as an insert into a stage play) scarcely surpasses the original dimensions of *verbunkos* dance, but constitutes a significant attempt to create a Hungarian declamation.

József Kossovits's melody
to Mihály Csokonai Vitéz's poem, entitled "To Hope".
In Szabolcsi, B.: Handbook of the History of Hungarian Music,
Collection of Examples, No. X/3c.

(Celestial phenomenon, playing with mortals...)

Antal Csermák (*c.* 1774–1822) composed a programmatic string quartet (Impending Danger), which, despite its rather short movements, takes a step towards the independent treatment of motifs. Apart from character pieces which were Hungarian in tone, written for piano, or chamber ensemble, the first widely recognized results appeared in the field of opera. The Hungarian-style overtures, ensembles, arias and ballets in the operas of Ferenc Erkel are the complete equals of the "European" music in them.

4. Finally, the form that aimed highest was the integration of the idiom of *verbunkos* into the composer's individual vocabulary of expression, turning it into a style pervading his works, or his oeuvre, as a whole, and also appearing in the large forms. This was only fully achieved by Franz Liszt. But among the minor masters Mihály Mosonyi (1815–1870), a friend of Liszt's who came to Pest

from Pressburg, approximated most closely to this ideal. After his early works in a "German" style (symphonies, church music, chamber works and an opera), Mosonyi became the most ardent apostle of art music built out of Hungarian elements (cantatas, operas, and piano pieces).

Mosonyi, Mihály: Mourning Notes on the Death of István Széchenyi,
in Szabolcsi, B.: Handbook of the History of Hungarian Music,
Collection of Examples, No. XIII/4.

Composers

But for most composers of the first half of the nineteenth century, works in a Hungarian tone constitute only a minor part of their oeuvre. The list of these composers is longer than that just dealt with, and the catalogue of their works often bespeaks an attempt to master the large-scale forms. In most cases a typical oeuvre will consist of long church works, symphonies, string quartets on the one hand, and short piano pieces, variations and suites in Hungarian style on the other. But the question to what extent these works represent a transition from the classical style towards some of the tendencies of Romanticism and how important their composers are, and how individual are their personalities, cannot be answered because their study, analysis and performance have hardly begun.

Early in the century church musicians must still have formed the most internationally oriented group of musicians, and the most highly qualified. Besides being engaged in church music, it was almost always due to them that the musical scene in the towns was so active, the organization of concerts, the performance of major works from abroad and the running of musical education and music societies. An excellent example of this type of musician was Antal Richter (*c*. 1802–1854) from Győr, who composed many church works and cantatas. His many colleagues of a similar stature include, for example, Georg

Lickl from Pécs (1769–1843), Ferenc Kemény (1763–1832), a mass in Hungarian style for male choir, and Hungarian choral works), and József Kleinmann (1775–1841) from Veszprém, Alajos Czibulka (1768–1845), József Seemann (1782–1839, masses, requiems, oratorios), and Ferenc Bräuer (1799–1864, a pupil of Hummel, oratorios, church works, choral pieces) from Pest, Antal Seyler (active in Pest-Buda and Esztergom between 1808–1841), and from smaller towns Tamás Gabrielli (1795–1858), Ferenc Limmer (1808–1857) and György Arnold (1781–1848).

Another group of composers comes from the world of performance. Urban musical life, theatres and orchestras gradually ensured then a livelihood, and even a career as a soloist, several being noted artist who toured abroad. Their works enriched not only the repertoire for their own instrument, but included chamber works and stage music. Almost all of them composed songs and choral pieces with Hungarian words. To mention a few names from this group: in Pozsony (Bratislava) Károly Winkler (1786–1844, virtuoso piano pieces) and János Batka (1795–1874), in Pécs Prosper Amtmann (1809–1854, flute concerto, songs, overtures) and Imre Weidinger, and in Pest the brothers Ferenc (1821–1883) and Károly (1825–1900) Doppler (operas and other stage works), the highly talented pianist Imre Székely (1823–1887, fugues, inventions, orchestral music, and Hungarian piano music), Lajos Bakody (1833–1902, organ sonata, symphony), and Károly Huber (1828–1885, operas, violin works and violin tutor).

By the nineteenth century teaching posts could also provide a livelihood for musicians, many of whom also composed. Among these were József Merkl (1811–1887, string quartet, sonata for violin and piano), Károly Thern (1817–1886), and the most important of them, Róbert Volkmann (1815–1883), a German-born romantic composer who worked in Pest between 1839 and 1875 (orchestral and chamber works, operas and songs).

Some amateur composers who had a musical education but did not earn their living as musicians are reveal in the output a remarkably wide sociological background of music culture. (Their works have not been studied so far.).They include Tádé Amadé (1783–1845), Miklós Földváry (1801–1837, piano pieces), István Prónay (1820–1892, a "Hungarian symphony"), and others. If to this one adds composers engaged in the organization of musical life and not attached to any given institution (such as János Pető, or András Bartay, who wrote operas, a mass, and an oratorio, as well as Hungarian dances and songs), together with a few minor masters who lived by composition, like János Spech (*c.* 1767–1836, cantata, mass, piano pieces, chamber works and Hungarian songs), then the number of composers is sufficient evidence of the vigorous beginnings of musical life among the middle-classes. Movement between countries was no longer a one-way process, several of the composers listed, as well as others, working for varying periods in Vienna or further west, thus acting as spreader of influence in both directions.

The Musical Theatre

A special place is occupied by theatre composers who were factotums of the stage. Sometimes they only re-worked music already composed, adapting it to local re-sources, sometimes they did orchestrations, and sometimes they wrote new additional songs, or even ventured into the field of opera.

In the early nineteenth century instead of guest com-panies from abroad there were Hungarian itinerant or per-manent companies, whose repertoire ranged from Hunga-rian and Austro-German *Singspiel*s (spoken dialogue interspersed with songs) to opera. They performed, for instance, works by Pergolesi, Dittersdorf and Mozart (in 1793, Pest audiences heard *The Magic Flute*). Between 1807 and 1814, the Kolozsvár (Cluj-Napoca) company gave the first local performances of twenty sung stage works (operas and musical plays) and ten ballets, while in 1812 the German theatre in Pest performed forty works (operas and *Singspiels*).

The manager of the Pest theatre, Alajos Czibulka (1768–1846) was a trained musician (for a time working as a church choirmaster) who composed songs and dances. Franz Xaver Kleinheinz (1765–1832), Vincenz Ferrarius Tuczek (1755–c. 1820), Johann Gallus Mederitsch (1752–1835), Franz Roser (1779–1830) and other theatre composers from abroad prepared the way for the first Hungarian Singspiels (József Chudy: *Prince Pikko*, 1793, and József Ruzitska: *Béla's Flight*, 1822). The brothers Doppler, from Lemberg, were also prolific composers.

During the first period there were two possible directions: to follow international operatic practice or to use short Hungarian song inserts. The spirit of the age increasingly favoured the latter, particularly when stage plays themselves turned from the great international themes to Hungarian actuality (or what was believed to be actual). When subjects considered to be popular reached the stage, so as to arouse the wide enthusiasm of audiences, they bowed to the populistic trend prevailing in literature. These plays, called *népszínmű* (about "Hungarian" village life with musical interludes) required the addition of songs. What made an aria "Hungarian" to the composer and his audience was determined–within fairly narrow boundaries–by the taste for *verbunkos* style and "folk-style" composed songs. But it was just these boundaries that prevented any development of a wider formal span, larger-scale musical ideas, or a truly operatic intonation.

The only composer who wanted to put an end to this contradiction, and resolve it in a synthesis, was Ferenc Erkel (1810–1893). Despite his successful work however it was clear that the paths of opera and Hungarian *Singspiel*, which in the early period of Hungarian theatre existed side by side, were now parting for good. By the second half of the century, opera came increasingly to follow the international current (Gusztáv Fáy, Bódog Pichler, Gusztáv Bőhm, Ödön Mihalovich), while the *Singspiel* floundered in the deficiencies of music and taste in the *népszínmű*.

Ferenc Erkel

The family of Ferenc Erkel* came from Pozsony (Bratislava) County, though he himself was born in the other end of the country, where his father was a teacher and choirmaster. After spending some years in Pozsony (Bratislava), in Kolozsvár (Cluj-Napoca) and with an aristocratic

---

* Ferenc Erkel was born in 1810 in Gyula, into an old-established family of musicians in the Pozsony region. His first teacher of the piano was his father, schoolmaster at Gyula and director of the church choir. During his grammar school years in Pozsony, Erkel studied music under Henrik Klein, later continuing his studies at Kolozsvár, where he also gave concerts and came into contact with the musical theatre. From 1834 he lived as a pianist in Pest (giving the first performances there of works by Chopin, Beethoven, Moscheles, Thalberg, etc.). He became deputy conductor in a theatre and later the chief conductor of the Hungarian National Theatre, where he conducted the European opera repertoire of the day, training outstanding singers. From 1854 he was the chief conductor of the Philharmonic Society, and from 1884, the chief musical director of the Opera House. In 1875 he as appointed director of the Academy of Music, where he also taught the piano. He died in 1893 in Budapest. His operas include: *Mária Báthori, László Hunyadi, Ban Bánk, Sarolta, György Dózsa, György Brankovics, Anonymous Heroes,* and *King Stephen.* He also wrote incidental music for plays, orchestral variations, choral works, Hungarian-style chamber music and piano works.

family, in 1835 Erkel went to Pest where he became the musical director of the National Theatre. He organized and expanded the orchestra of the theatre, breaking with the former assorted repertoire, performing instead the standard European operas. He also performed piano concertos and other piano works, as well as conducting concerts. Erkel was the first Hungarian musician of his day to embody the full significance of what it means to be a professional. It was typical that, when towards the end of his life he became a teacher at the Academy of Music, he urged his pupils to concentrate on simplicity and purity, and insisted on the sound foundations of the profession instead of wanton virtuosity. At the same time his activity created a free artistic spirit which determined the atmosphere of Hungarian higher musical education as a whole.

Erkel's work as a composer concentrated on the theatre. The list of his stage works is only supplemented by Hungarian-style piano pieces and choral pieces written to support the choral movement. His works for the stage on the other hand from incidental music, ballets and entre-actes via occasional compositions, sometimes written in collaboration with other composers, to grand operas that brought him national fame and success.

His first opera was *Mária Báthori*, premiered in 1840, in which he only occasionally blended the German-Italian style with Hungarian stylistic elements. The overture, however, is considered to be the first attempt at the creation of Hungarian symphonic music. Real success came in 1844, with the premiere of *László Hunyadi*. A component of this success was the political topicality of the libretto: the historical subject of the opera (the tragedy of a young fifteenth century nobleman who fell victim to a political plot) meant for the Hungarian national movement on the path to revolution what Verdi's *Nabucco* meant for Italy. But beyond this, it was also generally felt that, after the many dilettante compositions, here was a widely experienced composer who was capable of giving musical expression to the eloquence of the Hungarian language, and of composing the first Hungarian full-length opera. The popularity of the opera was evidenced not only by the succession of performances (at Arad, Nagyvárad, Temesvár/, Gyula, Kolozsvár, Kassa, Miskolc and Pozsony), but by the inclusion of extracts in the repertoire of military and gypsy bands, through them even reaching folk-music. Alongside its Hungarian stylistic features, and rhythm *László Hunyadi* also brought to the Hungarian stage the traditions of German and Italian opera.

Erkel. F.: Hunyadi László. 7.

Óh, szállj hoz- zám,

ég an - gya - la, osz - lasd az éj - nek

gyász - bo - rú - ját,   óh, Má - ri - ám,

na - pom   te vagy,   á - raszd a haj - nal

fény - su - ga - rát,   az aj - ki - don   van

an - nak bí - bo-ra   (etc.)

(O fly to me,
heavenly angel, dissolve the mourning grief of the night,
O my Maria, you are my sun, radiate the light of dawn,
whose purple is on your lips...)

Erkel did not forget what he had learned from teachers like Henrik Klein, with their West European cultural background, and in his works is to be found everything he learned as a pianist and a conductor from the works of the great masters. In this way he was equipped to go beyond the musical attempts of his predecessors in the theatre. He deliberately tried to depict the emotional characterization of the various scenes by mixing the various styles. This is how in his next opera, *Ban Bánk*, first performed in 1861, he came to use alternately "antique", "contrapuntal", "brilliant", French, Italian, and in some scenes expressly Hungarian styles. The premiere of *Ban Bánk* was perhaps even more successful than that of *Hunyadi*. The libretto, based on the most important Hungarian play of the first half of the nineteenth century, by József Katona, is about the leader of a conspiracy of the barons in the thirteenth century against overbearing foreign powers in the country. This times even those critics who previously had had their doubts, surrendered. The next years saw performances in quick succession both in Pest and throughout the country.

Erkel's truly imperishable composition, however, is the

Hungarian national anthem, composed to a poem by an outstanding poet of the day, Ferenc Kölcsey (1844). Erkel felt that for this exceptional task he should not yield to the temptations of a folk-style or *verbunkos*-type Hungarian-ness, as did the other composers who entered the compe-tition held for an anthem. He used a more timeless, reserved and abstract musical idiom–according to a con-temporary source, drawing inspiration from his memories of the peels of bells–to produce the melody that was to be accepted by all layers of society down the centuries as their very own.

Erkel. F.-Kölcsey. F.: Anthem.

Is - ten,áldd meg   a ma-gyart   jó kedvvel bő - ség - gel,

Nyújts fe - lé - je   vé - dő kart,   ha küzd el - len - ség - gel,

Bal - sors a - kit   ré - gen tép,   hozz rá víg esz - ten-dőt,

Meg - bűnhőd-te   már e nép a   múl- tat s jö - ven - dőt.

(God bless the Hungarians with good spirits and plenty, extend a protecting hand to them when they fight their enemies. Long torn by ill fate, grant them happy days, this people has already stoned for its past and future.)

Although Ban Bánk was followed by a succession of new works (*Sarolta* in 1862, *György Dózsa* in 1867, *György Brankovics* in 1874, *Anonymous Heroes* in 1880 and *King Stephen* in 1885), Erkel wrote them with growing inner uncertainty, and a sense of exploration. One should in fact, speak rather of works written by his sons, using their father's sketches, and pretending them under his name. In these works an increased role is assigned to Hungarian-style declamation, and a larger proportion of Hungarian motifs draw from the *verbunkos* tradition.

The desire for opera consisting of purely Hungarian elements was stressed at the time by Mihály Mosonyi, while the strengthening of operatic declamation shows rather the influence of Wagner, perhaps mainly through Erkel's sons. To unite such heterogeneous stylistic elements into a modern, artistic synthesis called for a deeply meditating compositional faculty. Only the genius of Franz Liszt could bring about this synthesis.

Franz Liszt and Hungary

Franz Liszt (1811–1886)* was the first Hungarian whose genius took him beyond the confines of the country's musical culture to assume universal significance. This, however, did not serve to dissociate him from Hungarian mu-

---

* Franz Liszt was born at Doborján (Raiding-Unterfrauenhaid) in 1811. His father was a steward to the Esterházy family and the first piano teacher of his son. The boy began to make public appearances playing the piano at the age of eight. In Vienna he studied under Czerny and Salieri. Encouraged by the boy's successes in Pozsony, Vienna and Pest, in 1823 his father took him to Paris. He studied composition and earned great acclaim with his piano performances and improvisations, both in France and England. He taught the piano and was in touch with the notabilities of the world of literature and composition. In 1835 he settled in Geneva, and from 1836 appeared as a celebrated travelling concert pianist. He first returned to his native country in 1838 on a concert tour, which also marked the beginning of an international career of ten years as a virtuoso pianist. After 1847 he settled in Weimar, which he turned into a musical centre with the appearances of noted artists and their works. He himself was a zealous performer of new compositions of the Romantic repertoire (particularly Wagner's works). In 1860 he moved to Rome, where he worked at the revival of Catholic church music. In 1865 he took minor orders in the Church, from then onwards residing alternately between Rome, Weimar, and Pest. He took an active part in Hungarian musical life and was a generous supporter of musical foundations. He died in Bayreuth in 1886. Here we can only give a selection

sical culture, instead, over the years he increasingly established conscious links with the country's life as a man, a
musician and a composer. Here, of course, we shall approach his career only from this angle, discussing those
aspects which form part of the history of Hungarian music.

Liszt was born at Doborján (Raiding-Unterfrauenhaid),
in Sopron County, the area with the most highly developed
musical life in Hungary. His musical education was begun
by his father, Ádám Liszt, who was steward on the Esterházy estates. For some time Ádám played the cello in the
Esterházy orchestra, and was acquainted with Haydn and
Hummel, playing many important works of the period. The
future of the child was decided in the palace of the Pozsony
(Bratislava) branch of the Esterházy family: five Hungarian magnates donated a scholarship towards his studies.
Even though the amount did not fully cover the costs, it
gave enough encouragement to the father to take the risk
of moving with the child to Vienna. Czerny, a pupil of
Beethoven, undertook to teach the gifted boy, who was
still unpolished musically and technically. The child
studied singing and theory under Antonio Salieri, his first
composition being published when he was 11 years old
by Diabelli. Before Ádám Liszt set out on a concert tour
with his son in Western Europe, the 12-year-old child
played in Pest and was given a fervent reception. "He will

---

of some of his most significant compositions. Vocal works: *Die Legende
von der heiligen Elisabeth* (1857–62), *Christus* (1862–67), masses,
requiem, *Via Crucis*, a large number of sacred and secular choral works.
Orchestral works: *Tasso* (1849–54), *Les Préludes* (1848–54), *Orpheus*
(1853–54), *Mazeppa* (1851–54), *Hungaria* (1854), *Hamlet* (1858) and
other symphonic poems. *Faust Symphony* (1854), *Dante Symphony*
(1855–56), *Piano Concerto in E flat major* (1849–53), *Piano Concerto
in A major* (1839–61), *Totentanz* (1849–59). A great number of piano
works, including *Années de pelerinage*, *Hungarian Historical Portraits*,
Nineteen Hungarian Rhapsodies, *Mephisto*, *Waltzes*, *Csárdás obstiné*,
Bagatelle Without Tonality, etc. Piano transcriptions, organ works, songs.

bring great glory to his native country through his career as an artist," the press wrote. His concert repertoire included, alongside virtuoso pieces and extemporizations, also Hungarian works, the Rákóczi March, and transcriptions of Csermák, Lavotta and Bihari, from Mohaupt's collection mentioned already. Even as a small child, he listened with keen attention to the playing of the wandering gypsy musicians at Doborján.

In Paris he entered a new expanding world. His concert tours, which followed one another in quick succession, acquainted him with every possible form of success. He was the friend of noted musicians, leading writers, philosophers, painters and public figures, and got to know all the major compositions and musical trends of his day. While playing the piano and composing, he wrote, reflected and thought on a global scale.

The great Pest flood of 1838 made him realize for the first time where he really belonged. He went to help his compatriots by giving charity concerts. Even more important perhaps than this fine gesture was what took place internally in Liszt. "I had got accustomed to thinking of France as my country, and did not think that I had another country as well..." Luckily for music at large and Hungarian music also, this realization was not followed by a spectacular conversion. Liszt remained to the end of his life what he had always been: a musician who thought, felt, and made music in a universal content, whose white hot activity incorporated everything and everybody in Europe. It was precisely this under musical spotlight that he could bring to bear on the musical material offered by his native land, material which Liszt, moved by warm patriotic emotion but still viewing its potentialities with the eye of a musician, incorporated into his art.

He gave charity concerts in Vienna for Hungarians there, returning to his "wild and remote" country only at

the end of 1839. His first concert in Hungary was in Pozsony (Bratislava), and when he arrived in Pest he was
welcomed by a cantata. At Liszt's request the concert tickets were printed only in Hungarian, but he was able to
reply to the welcome speeches only in French. At the end
of his concert tour early in 1840, when he was girded with
a sword of honour, a scene he described in the letter quoted
earlier, he said: "This sword, once so powerfully
flourished in the defence of the fatherland, has now been
entrusted to weak and peaceful hands. Is this not a symbol?
Do you perhaps wish to say by this that Hungary, after
having won so many triumphs in the battle field, now seeks
glory in the arts, literature and science, the friends of
peace?" Liszt's was a triumphal progress: he was granted
honorary citizenship of Pest, and welcomed with unflag-
ging enthusiasm in Győr, Pozsony (Bratislava), his native
village of Doborján (Raiding-Unterfrauenhaid) and in Kismarton (Eisenstadt) and Sopron.

    Liszt then embarked once again on the life of a virtuoso
pianist, travelling ceaselessly, and only in 1846 did he return to Hungary. Here he again met István Széchenyi, a
mutual esteem existing between the two men (twenty years
later Liszt wrote one of his finest piano pieces to the death
of Széchenyi). He began to take an interest in Hungary's
musical life and got to know Hungarian musicians and
their works. After only a few months, he conducted the
overture to Erkel's opera *Hunyadi* in Vienna. He was ex-
cited by Hungary's song tradition, and thought of collecting the songs of the gypsies, thinking them to be Hungarian
music. Even when we know that he only encountered the
fashionable Hungarian popular song (*nóta*) of his day, still
it was sufficient to stimulate him towards solving his problems as a composer. In 1846, he toured the southern regions of Hungary and after several concerts in Transylvania, continued his way eastwards. The failure of the War

of Independence led him to write funeral composition. The 1850s saw a strengthening of his Hungarian connections. He sent his pupil, Hans von Bülow to Pest with detailed instructions concerning whom he should meet. He replied to the famous poet Mihály Vörösmarty's ode to him with a symphonic poem: *Hungaria.*

In 1855, Liszt was commissioned to compose a mass for the dedication of the new cathedral at Esztergom. He worked enthusiastically on the mass, whose boldness and new features sprang from an innermost change both in Liszt's attitude and in his music, astonishing many of his earlier supporters. After long procrastination the mass was finally performed not only in Esztergom but also in Pest. "Yesterday my mass was given a prodigious performance in the City Church of Pest, which could hardly contain the huge crowd of interested listeners." During his visit to Hungary that year he gave several charity concerts for re-ligious organizations and the promotion of musical culture which now became a regular custom, even if aside from such occasions, he had ended his career as a pianist. In 1858, he was again in Hungary, at which time he came into closer contact with the choral movement. In 1859, his book on gypsies was published turning wide sections of the press against him. "Shall I put it in words? The uproar surrounding my volume on the gypsies made me feel that I am a much truer Hungarian than my adversaries, the would-be Magyars..."

Liszt's personal links nevertheless continued to strengthen with Hungarian musical events and musicians (Mosonyi, then later members of the younger generation including Mihalovich, Zichy, Ábrányi, etc.). After 1870, Liszt spent a growing amount of time in Hungary, dividing his time each year between Rom, Weimar and Pest. He set up a permanent home in Pest, and followed with keen attention the concert life in the city, premieres and the

work done by musical societies and choirs. The former
emperor of music now rehearsed with the girls' choir in
the school run by nuns of the Institute of the Blessed Virgin
Mary... (the so-called English Sisters). The 1870s saw a
plan to found an Academy of Music, with Liszt to be
elected as its president. At first Liszt was reluctant, as he
felt the project to be not sufficiently thought out, but eventually undertook the post, in the years to come developing
the piano department with great zeal, while in his capacity
as president he helped choose teaching staff of a high-standard. (For a long time the Academy of Music functioned
in Liszt's Pest apartments.) Liszt's pupils included István
Thomán, later the piano teacher of Bartók, and it was at
Liszt's suggestion that János Koessler was appointed a
teacher, later teaching composition to Bartók and Kodály.
There is practically no musical institution in modern Hungary that at the time of its formation would not have had
the goodwill and attentive support of Liszt.

It is not easy to draw lines between the various mani-
festations of Liszt's "Hungarian" pieces in his different
creative periods. His first Hungarian fantasias still date
from the chronological period of his Romantic output of
virtuoso piano pieces and transcriptions. Liszt, receptive
to every effect and unsurpassed master of the piano, paid
tribute in them to his native country, at the same time incorporating into his own musical world the Hungarian
style. If we were unaware of his childhood experiences
and the patriotic promptings that sparked off these works,
we might perhaps see in them nothing more than another
sign of an appetite to engulf everything that came his way,
through which he reworked poems, paintings, foreign
styles, pieces and musical experiences into his own works.
If Auber, Bellini, Donizetti and Paganini could provide
raw material for Liszt's imagination, why not the same for
the Rákóczi march or the fashionable Hungarian popular

songs and dances of the time? His *Heroischer Marsch in Ungarischen Styl* or the *Ungarischer Sturmmarsch* exist side by side with his galops and waltzes. They are European pieces, which from a musical point of view treat the Hungarian motif almost as a happy find. The broad formation, elegant handling of the instrument and easy, effortless worldliness of these sets of fantasias composed from Hungarian songs and dances turned them into works accepted in international concert life. And although incomparably better in their execution, and filtered through the imagination of a gifted artist, nonetheless these pieces are still the successors to the Hungarian-style dance suites of the late eighteenth century.

A borderline between periods can be drawn around 1850. Losing nothing of his attainment, his varigated world of harmony, his feeling for instruments, Liszt became a deeper composer in these years. He broke off his concert tours and his sets of "success-seeking compositions" and turned wholeheartedly toward the task of exploration as a composer. He abandoned the practical role of his music which was harnessed to the acclaim of Liszt the concert pianist. It was the beginning of the period of the great symphonic poems and symphonies, the mysterious piano pieces, the setting out on a voyage of exploration, the church works and oratorios that transformed Liszt's style.

The style became more concise, the content conveyed by a firm structure. Their tonal world was expanded on the one hand by elements derived from the modal turns of early music, and on the other by many various juxtapositions of the twelve notes which became increasingly equal in rank. Different relationships were formed between keys which earlier had been separate, even distant tonalities, because directly linked the individual notes assuming an independent role. Alongside this earlier formal patterns were replaced by individual structures built on the logic of the developing musical idea. The single-movement sonata, symphony and concerto became the symbol and appropriate framework of this self-determining development.

In this context, the elements of Liszt's "Hungarian" inheritance also take on a new meaning. Intellectually, in that in obedience to the moral imperative of his intimate links with Hungarian history, events and persons, and with the historical Hungarian nation, he abandoned the scintillating "national" mood and wrote pieces reflecting the fate of the nation (e.g. *Funerailles*, to commemorate the tragic events of 1849, the symphonic poem *Hungaria*, or the *Missa solemnis*, written for the consecration of the Esztergom basilica). And musically in that these elements bring something new: works whose themes and character consciously approach Hungarian reality, increasingly incorporate organically Hungarian rhythmic elements, motifs and a characteristic use of intervals into their fabric, conceived still essentially in the spirit of high Romanticism. Instead of a surface presence of melodic quotations or character, the Hungarian elements sink deeper into the composer's individual style, where they unite to produce Liszt's modern musical idiom.

Liszt, F.: Sunt lacrymae rerum.

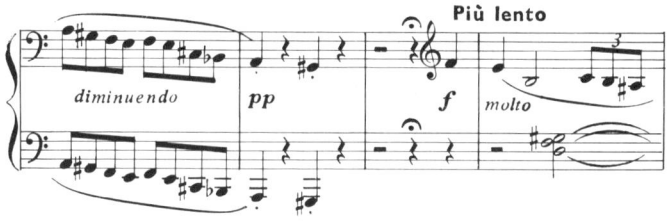

As borne out by *Mosonyi's Trauermarsch*, the *Hungarian Historical Portraits*, *Dem Andenken Petőfis*, the *Ungarisches Königslied*, and a whole range of similar works, Liszt's conscious acceptance of his Hungarianness did not fade during the last twenty years of his life, but rather became more intense. More important is the evidence of his musical development irrespective of any Hungarian reference in the title. The Hungarian precedents in his music also contributed to Liszt's style becoming increasingly reduced, concentrating more on the essence. At the same time the fabric built out of these basic elements became richer and more meaningful. We see a musical development in the opposite direction to his earlier style, in some senses even to that of his Romantic contemporaries, and which prepared the way for the twentieth century. Liszt's new ear which could unite Gregorian chant, Palestrina, Bach, Classicism and Romanticism, also embodied the "national" elements tried out in his Hungarian works, confronting them with his universal inheritance. This synthesis was not a matter of adding elements to each other but of grasping their common root problems. For example, scales which in the nineteenth century were considered Hungarian became melodic devices used to overstep the bounds of classical tonality and to elaborate enharmonic relationships.

All the rhythmic intervallic and melodic elements in Liszt's works are to be found in the works of Mihály Mosonyi and his contemporaries, but lacking Liszt's synthesizing compositional imagination. Classical harmony and form and the *verbunkos* inheritance mutually impede one another. In Liszt, the organic construction, the developing large harmonic structure moving increasingly away from the major-minor system, the increasing importance and autonomy of the single note, all in the presence of a sovereign musical idea give these works a universal value in musical history. Their spirit is purely European imbibing everything, yet surpassing everything produced earlier. How did this come to include–not as colouring but as a creative force–Hungarian motives whose Hungarian character and application in art music gave rise earlier to our justified misgivings?

Liszt in fact reduces this style, or rather manner, to its components viewing it from the point of view of his modern musical programme evident in his early youth, and which propelled him the more vehemently the older he became. The works of minor composers of the period are often coloured by the Hungarian scale,–though derived from the classical manner of hearing them. An important part is played in these by the augmented second–the glittering emblem of *verbunkos* music–the sharpened fourth degree with the natural seventh, and the diminished fourth that lies between the sharpened seventh degree and the minor third. The presence of these is undoubtedly the symbol of "Hungarian" commitment in Liszt as well. But they become at the same time a device for augmenting tonal relationships, for developing interval structures that transcend keys, and for the organization of a now larger empire. These were tasks common to all the composers of late Romanticism. Liszt, however, did not bring this about artificially but sifted it as it were, from the "Hungarian" motifs, from the basic melodic material. Thus the presence of these intervals in the final analysis leads his imagination towards a uniform treatment of the twelve notes, the individualizing (punctuating) of single notes, in short towards the tonal revolution of the twentieth century, but not speculatively, instead, naturally.

The development evident in Liszt's late works also presents us with interesting general lesson. The incorporation of *verbunkos* elements had the same effect on his thinking as did his acquaintanceship with early European music. Twentieth century scholars know that the *verbunkos* style is an eighteenth century practice that came about and grew into vogue under singular influences. But for art music the key issue was not its authenticity. Ardent Hungarian composers who used it failed to create a "world-conquering Hungarian art music" not because it was not sufficiently Hungarian–as has been claimed by zealous ethnomusicologists of our day. The basic question was whether modern, late Romantic musical material could be amalgamated with a style which in many respects was alien to it (with its small-scale forms and narrow harmonic and tonal system) and if so how. This type of task is what divides– necessarily it seems–the paths of minor and great composers. In the hands of the former the foreign material remains simply an atmospheric tingeing. For the great ones this polarity sets off a relentless process of dismantling, leading to a deeper acquaintenceship with the material. At the same time, the synthesis of the styles, if in the course of this process they reach a stage suitable for synthesis, offers an opportunity to create a new style and a firmer structural amalgam. The result is something whose overall effect may radiate pure spirituality, and a seriousness pointing beyond the music.

Was Liszt Hungarian? One could hardly ask a more fruitless question. Liszt is a universal European figure, not confined to periods and nations. At the same time he is a genius who was enriched by, and who enriches Hungarian music. He declared himself to be Hungarian, whilst incorporating the whole of European culture into his thinking. Liszt occupies a place between Paris, Rome, Weimar and Pest–French Romanticism, Catholicism, German culture and the Hungarian Academy of Music. This is not a matter of what language one speaks or the geneology of one's parents.

Musical Institutions

The history of nineteenth century Hungarian music was perhaps more successful in the field of organizing musical institutions and developing a functioning musical life than in the field of composition.

The growth of private concerts and "academies" in the eighteenth century led to the development of modern public concerts. Pozsony (Bratislava) and Pest were soon followed by the provincial towns, and from the 1830s and '40s onwards concerts of miscellaneous pieces were replaced by carefully compiled concert programmes, including the gems of Viennese Classicism and early Romanticism (Cherubini, Rossini, Meyerbeer, Bellini).

Concert life was boosted by newly formed musical societies, which became the centres of city musical life. They encouraged musical education, the acquisition of scores and the organization of choirs, and also provided opportunities for direct contact between local audiences and professional musicians.

We have already seen the role played by the musical theatre. The opera department of the National Theatre, which opened in 1837, provided a fairly rich repertoire with a permanent orchestra and a company of high-standard vocalists. After lengthy preliminaries, the department became independent in September 1884, when the Opera House with Erkel as the director, was opened with a gala performance of single acts from *Ban Bánk* and *Lohengrin*. Based on the theatre orchestra, the Philharmonic Society began (1867), being the city's first concert orchestra, for a long time remaining the main buttress of concert life in Budapest.

The new active concert life brought with it a rapid development in the art of performance, and the appearance of virtuoso soloists. It was chiefly Hungarian violinists who won recognition beyond the country's borders (Ede Reményi, József Bőhm, József Joachim), though some singers, too, appeared as admired guest artist in the great opera houses of the world (Kornélia Hollósy, Rozália Geizler).

After the early beginnings in the eighteenth century, there developed a full network of musical education, its foundations provided by societies, private teachers and music school run by the towns. (An article of 1826 mentions ten municipal music schools by name, disregarding the "unbelievably large number" of music schools functioning in church schools, girls' convent schools, and private teachers). The singing school of Pest, founded in 1840, was expanded, with the inclusion of instrumental teaching, into the National Music School, with several hundred pupils and eminent teachers, most of whom were also active as well known performers or composers. The crowning event of this growth was the opening of the Hungarian National Royal Academy of Music (today the Liszt Ferenc Academy of Music), with Liszt as the president and Erkel the director.

The comprehensive network of choral societies also played a major role in the spread of musical culture. Although their repertoire was often restricted to pleasant homophonic choral pieces, the members of these amateur choirs–operating as church groups, voluntary groups and societies–formed the most receptive concert audiences. (In Pécs alone the society had 38 singing and 346 supporting members in 1862.) Their importance was recognized by professional musicians who followed their activities with keen interest (national singing festivals), while the best composers (Erkel, Liszt, Mosonyi) were always happy to write works for them.

All this was supplemented by the the increasingly regular appearance of music-educational literature, the growth in the musical instrument-making, the printing of music, publications on musical aesthetics and a growing musical press (Zenészeti Lapok–Musical Gazette, begun in 1860), together with the work of scholars in musicology and musical historiography (Gábor Mátray, István Bartalus and Mihály Bogisich).

The End of the Century

By the 1870s, Budapest had become the centre of an advanced musical life, linked to cities in Germany and Austria exchanges of visiting musicians. One to the artistic and organizing work of Erkel and his son Sándor, alongside the traditional opera and concert repertoire, works by contemporary composers (Brahms, Wagner, Liszt and Verdi) were also regularly given in Budapest, sometimes under the baton of the composer himself. The work of three successive eminent conductors guaranteed high standards: János Richter (the son of the cathedral choir director Antal Richter, a friend of Liszt and Wagner, and later conductor of the Manchester Hallé Orchestra, who gave the premiere of Bartók's *Kossuth Symphony*), Gustav Mahler (chief conductor of the Budapest Opera House from 1888 to 1891) and Artúr Nikisch. Against this background performance standards were also raised to international levels, both as regards orchestral playing (many players still coming from abroad and establishing the musical standards) and soloists (Lipót Auer, Jenő Hubay and Géza Zichy, all artists of European repute who travelled extensively). Performing traditions were handed down from generation to generation via the National Music School, and particularly the Academy of Music, which, under the purposeful direction of Ödön Mihalovich, engaged a long line of eminent musicians and teachers from both Hungary and abroad.

The shortcomings lay in three areas. Firstly, although a colorful musical scene developed in the provinces due to societies of music-lovers, chamber groups formed by amateurs, and concert promoting associations, the personalities guaranteeing the form and standards of modern musical life were too much concentrated in Budapest. Secondly, the majority of the middle classes still did not appreciate serious music, hiding their lack of culture behind national slogans: hence musical life lacked a broad base. And thirdly, Kodály's condemnation also applied: "The extremely thin layer of those people with any musical cultivation were nourished only by a cult of masterpieces of foreign origin, expressing German or Italian mentality and grown to international proportions. Hungarian character in higher music they only recognized, with some condescension, in Erkel's operas and Liszt's rhapsodies. From the lack of success of other, isolated attempts, they mostly reached the conviction that Hungarian music of a higher artistic character remained only a dream".

Yet the musicians of a higher culture cannot be blamed for an indifference towards the Hungarian character of the nation's music. It was rather that the "Hungarian" music which 60 or 70 yars previously had been expected to become a great art music, now, after encountering the great works of late Romanticism, appeared to be unable to bear the burden. This resulted in a certain hesitancy and dejection in Hungarian composition at the end of the century.

It is also possible that some trained composers attached greater importance to keeping abreast with general progress and worked in the spirit of, or perhaps as the epigons of German Romanticism. The best of these was Károly Goldmark (1830–1915). Born in Keszthely, Goldmark studied in Hungary and worked in Vienna. His operas are an individual blend of several traditions (this being particularly true for *Die Königin von Saba*–The Queen of Sheba), and along with his overtures, a violin concerto and chamber music, contain music which has remained a living force to the present day.

˙ In the larger forms, creative strength is most clearly evident in the field of opera (Sándor Erkel 1846–1900, Ferenc Rákosi 1855–1913, Aladár Radó 1882-1914, etc.). Worthy of mention is the fact that Hungarian operetta, which achieved success world-wide, originated from the joint influence of Hungarian opera and the lighter Viennese genres (Ferenc Lehár 1870–1948, Imre Kálmán 1882–1953, Jenő Huszka 1875–1960).

Among the composers who incorporated late Romanticism into his music the most notable was Ödön Mihalovich (1842–1929) mentioned above. A close friend of Liszt, Wagner and von Bülow, he followed in their wake, writing operas, four symphonies, overtures, songs and choral works. Also embarking on their careers at the turn of the century were several, highly skilled and talented members of a new generation, including Ernő Dohnányi (1877–1960), the eminent composer and pianist.

Another solution was sought by some minor composers, who employed a Hungarian intonation in short character pieces, "idylls" and programmatic mood music, being affected by Liszt and Romanticism only this framework (for example Károly Agghtázy, 1855–1915). Sometimes these composers typically followed the international style in their larger works, paying their tribute to national music in short character pieces. An isolated initiative was that of the gifted Sándor Bertha (1843–1912), who moved to Paris but remained faithful in his music to his native land, and searched for ways to blend Hungarian motifs with drier, classical forms alien to Romanticism but perhaps more enduring (for example in his "Hungarian fugue"). The question raised in his music was to be answered by the succeeding generation.

Magyar nóta (Hungarian "Popular" Song)

What was considered as Hungarian by this generation–including Liszt in his Hungarian rhapsodies–was further extended, apart from the verbunkos tradition, by another repertory. Simultaneously with the early nineteenth century cultivation of folk-poetry in Europe, interest in "folk"* features also grew in Hungary, where it coincided with the national enthusiasm of the Reform Period. Through a naive identification of "folk" with "national" hopes were alive that the former would lead to a knowledge of the latter. A positive result of this movement was that the collection of folk-music and folk-poetry began in the 1830s and 1840s, for the most part in an unprofessional manner, taking byways not highways.

Because this interest remained unorganized in both its principles and its methods it did not arrive at a knowledge of real folk music. "Folk" at this time simply meant "popular", or what was known generally, especially by the literati, the gentry and minor land owners, who made up the main body of the "folk" movement. For them "folksong" which chiefly meant the simpler among the eighteenth-century student songs. These, however, they regarded as being so much their own that they saw nothing reproachable in varying and reshaping the repertory themselves, or expanding it with new pieces in the same manner. For them the "people" did not mean a scientifically defined category, the opposite was a "foreigner", the opposite of folk-song being any music exceeding the length of a song. "Coming from the people", "written for the people", being of "popular (folk) character" were characteristics intermingling and not separated from one another. Musical illiteracy and Hungarianness were themselves sufficient reason for this broad layer to consider itself the "people" without further distinction, not only communally but individ-

---

* The German *volkslied* and Hungarian *népdal* are translated into English as folk-song. However, *volk* and *nép* mean *people*, hence the confusion between "folk and "popular" in the English translation *Nóta* means Hungarian nineteenth-century composed song in the supposed style of the "people".

ually as well, and thus to increase the "mass of folk-songs" with its own inventions. This, of course had nothing to do with real composition, most of the "creators" being unable to note down their songs whose notation and accompaniments were the work of the lower strata of musicians.

This new genre, the nineteenth century composed Hungarian popular song (*magyar nóta*) does undoubtedly have a community character. First of all, the songs are not individual creations, but rather the transformation of existing ones (which in fact led to many lawsuits regarding plagiarism, in itself an absurdity in the case of "folk"-songs) or a re-stringing together of familiar motifs. Also the composer had a community behind him which accepted and spread his work. New songs were distributed in handwriting or in print, and their addressees–the hundreds of composers of the songs–greated them with jubilation, praising them with superlatives. The people who by the second half of the century used and championed the *magyar nóta* were the new middle classes made up of the former landed gentry the white-collar intelligentsia and citizens nearly adopting Magyar ways, though it was also popular among the lower strata of city-dwellers and the upper strata of village people.

No matter how much the *magyar nóta* was built on variation, its style itself underwent some changes over a period of time. The starting point as mentioned already, was the eighteenth century students' songs, which in the nineteenth century gave way to a demand for "popularity", meaning simplicity. This layer of the Hungarian *nóta* was the most solid one stylistically.

Károly Thern's song, in Kerényi, Gy.: Volkstümliche Lieder, No. 33.

Ezt   a   ke- rek   er - dőt   já - rom   én,
Ezt   a   bar - na   kis - lányt   vá - rom   én,
Ez a   bar - na   kis - lány   vi - o - la,
Én   va-gyok a   vi - gasz - ta - ló - ja.

(Round and round this forest I go,
this little brunette I wait for.
This little brunette is a violet,
and I am to console her.)

Folk-music features evident in the first folk-song publications–though superficial–and vocal adaptations of verbunkos music modified this style only to a small extent. A fashion for lengthy, sentimental tunes relying on romantic harmony brought a great change, bringing an expression of individual, indeed exhibitionistic attitudes. At this point the *Magyar nóta* which until then could only be condemned for its emptiness and its power to distract people from what was better, turned into a force inimical to good taste.

Song by Kozák, G. and Sz. Nagy, E.,
in Sárosi. B.: Cigányzene (Gypsy Music). p. 167.

Nincsen olyan boldog ember, kinek szívét sose é- ri   bá - nat. . .   (

(There are no such happy people whose heart would never be touched by grief...)

The most effective medium for the spread of the *magyar nóta* was the gypsy band. Ever since their mass appearance in the eighteenth century, gypsy bands had no real repertoire of their own (least of all a gypsy repertoire). They played everything that pleased the merry-making public (in the twentieth century even fashionable dance music). Their playing uses special instrumental technique of ornamentation and performance, which in the best bands is developed to an admirable level. The Hungarian part of their repertoire rests on two pillars: *verbunkos* (in which they exhibit the best side of their tradition) and the two main forms of the Hungarian *nóta*: revelling and dance tunes, played with a technique that resembles verbunkos (*"csárdás"*) and sentimental sorrowful songs (*"hallgató"*–music for listening).

The New-style Hungarian Folk-song

"... and there was the third layer, the mysterious, unknown people of the village" (Kodály). During these very decades a veritable musical revolution was taking place in the villages: the development of the new-style Hungarian folk-song.

Its antecedents reach back to the late Middle Ages, when the first strophes with an "arched" construction appeared in the history of Hungarian melody (principally through church hymns). Sometimes the cadences are on the key note and the fifth, with fifth correspondencies between the first and the second lines. In the seventeenth and eighteenth centuries this type of form appears with growing frequency, including in secular songs as well, often combined with the return of the first line (formula AA⁵BA). Combined with this form is the use of the full seven degrees of the scale (heptatonic melody). Early in the nineteenth century a new element reinforces the fifth corre-

spondence: with its exact transposition in the second line,
a lengthier, more articulated first line, particularly in the
csárdás.

Parallel to this, as was demonstrated by Bartók, there
also took place a rhythmic transformation. The augmentation of the old swineherd's dance formula led to the development of slow, taut crotchets, with a free use of dotted
notes to fit the words, later with here and there crotchets
again fragmented into quavers.

These preparatory circumstances could lead to a new
style because they fitted into the traditions of Hungarian
folk-song. The opening lines became longer than in the
seventeenth-eighteenth century examples (with a syllable
count of 11-15 to the line) and filled with micromotifs and
interval links inherited from the old style, heptatonic scales
being realized by modal (Dorian, Mixolydian) melodies
and often even melodies stressing a pentatonic backbone.
Instead of the rigid correspondence of AA^5, a more flex-
ible form of ABBA (in the case of longer opening lines,
AABA) became predominant.

Folk-music collection, Berzence, Somogy County.

Jaj de ré - gen le - hul - lott a le - ve - le,

Ár - va ma - dár pár - ját ke - re - si ben - ne.

(Forest, forest, how high its top reaches up,
oh how long the leaves have dropped,
an orphaned bird seeks for its mate in it.)

Church hymns, the magyar nóta, ancient folk-song traditions and art-music impressions thus became synthesized into a completely different style. Almost all of its elements have their correspondences, sometimes even abroad, and yet, in their entirety they make an independent formation. And if it is true that one of the main criteria in the concept of folk-song is its ability to create homogeneous styles (Bartók), it is a veritable miracle that such a revolution could still took place at this time, directly after the complete collapse of folk culture.

The style embarked on its victorious career in the years between 1850 and 1900, beginning in the central region of the Hungarian linguistic area, in fact conquering the western and eastern counties as late as the middle of the twentieth century. The fact that it burnished into a uniform whole and spread throughout the country must have been due greatly to the new state of the peasantry, which after the liquidation of serfdom became more or less uniform and to their great migrations (common military service, seasonal casual labour with agricultural workers coming from different regions).

The details remain unknown to us even though they happened practically before our eyes. The upper classes remained unaware of the changes in folk-song just as they had been unaware of ancient Hungarian folk-music as a whole. By 1896, however, an ethnographer, Béla Vikár, set out to make phonograph recordings of classical old ballads and complaint-melodies from outlying little villages in Transylvania and bring them back to Budapest. Vikár was not a musician and his phonograph cylinders were simply shelved in the Ethnographic Museum. And while they waited for someone to break open the seal of their message, around them "Hungarian phantasies" were still being composed.

7 Hungarian Music in the 20th Century

In a letter about one of his first folk-song collecting tours, Bartók described the difficulties a collector had to face. The "traveller"–Bartók–requests "very old secular tunes" which the peasant woman could still learn from the old folk". She does not think he means it, saying that "the gentleman is only making fun of her". The collector shows her his notebook and quotes from songs he has obtained from others in the village. All in vain: "It does not become an old woman like me to have anything to do with secular songs like those, by now I can only remember holy songs." The collector hums the melody of a complaint has heard from other in the village as an example "You know this, don't you?" "I heard the song once, but I didn't learn it." Finally, at long last she starts singing a popular csárdás, saying: "Here, this is a very old song!' and goes on to offer a well-known Hungarian nóta (popular song), a comic chanson and a hymn, but she will not hear of any of the old ballads the collector asks for. Then, as Bartók puts it: "The traveller leaves broken-hearted. De capo al fine, morning to night, Monday to Sunday. It is unbearable. To hell with perseverance, endurance, patience. I'll go home ... you can't keep up this performance for more than six weeks. Even in my dreams I keep hearing fragments of it..." By the end of his life, however, in America, he remembers the times he spent among peasants in the villages as the happiest days of his life.

- The history of Hungary in the twentieth century is relatively well known. A few reminders will suffice: a lost world war–a bourgeois revolution turning into a communist revolution and followed by a counter-revolution (1918–1919)–the peace treaty of Versailles which deprived Hungary of two thirds of its territory and one third of its Hungarian-speaking population (1920)–conservative politics aimed at recovering the lost territories (Miklós Horthy's regime)–reannexation under the Munich and Vienna Accords of some of the territories with Hungarian inhabitants, and, the price paid for this, Hungary's entry into World War Two (delayed until 1941). Then attempts to withdraw from Hitler's side of the war–the German occupation of Hungary–peace treaty, again signed on the loser's side. Hungary now in the sphere of Soviet influence, introduction of the Stalinist form of socialism (1948)–uprising against Stalinism and for the country's independence (1956)–severe reprisals, followed by a slow economic and social development (from 1968). Growing economic difficulties and the slow progress of a reform period (1980's) leading to free, multy-party elections and a new coalition government (1990).

The Emergence of Béla Bartók and Zoltán Kodály

All the important developments in the history of twentieth-century Hungarian music are indissolubly associated with the work of Béla Bartók* (1881–1945) and Zoltán Kodály** (1882–1967). It seems only proper therefore to present this sketch of the period in relation to their activity.

Both Bartók and Kodály came to Budapest from the same region rich in musical traditions, namely Bartók came from Pozsony (Bratislava), and Kodály from Nagyszombat (Trnava). Both became pupils of János Koessler (composition) at the Academy of Music (Bartók also studied piano with István Thomán). Both arrived from music-playing middle-class families. Bartók's father was the principal of a Nagyszentmiklós school, played the piano and the cello, and ran an amateur orchestra. The child was first taught the piano by his mother, then continued his studies with the conductor of a church choir and the grammar school music teacher, though he must have taught himself first and foremost. When he was eleven he gave his first concert playing Beethoven's Waldstein Sonata. After moving to Pozsony (Bratislava), he played the piano a great deal, usually pieces making considerable demands, studied harmony, and gained benefit from the concerts and opera performances in the lively musical life of the city. According to his autobiography, "by the age of 18, I was quite well acquainted with the musical literature from Bach to Brahms." His first compositions (chamber music, piano pieces, songs) show the influence of Brahms. He entered the Academy of Music in 1899. He quickly made a name for himself, as a composer and an enthusiast of late German Romanticism (after Brahms, he was influenced by Wagner and Richard Strauss) and a highly accomplished pianist. He met Zoltán Kodály in the salon of Emma Sándor (later Kodály's wife).

---

* Béla Bartók was born in 1881 at Nagyszentmiklós (Sînnicolau Mare). His family were teachers, with musical inclinations. He studied at Nagyszöllős (Vinogradov) and Nagyvárad (Oradea), and first appeared in public as a pianist, including playing one of his own works, at a concert in 1892. From 1894 he studied in Pozsony (Bratislava) under László Erkel (Ferenc Erkel's son), and later with Antol Hyrtl. He appeared in public several times both as pianist and composer. From 1899 he attended the Academy of Music in Budapest. From 1903 he gave concerts in Germany and England. He first encountered authentic Hungarian folk-music in 1904–6, when he notated the many phonograph cylinders collected by Béla Vikár, and embarked on the collection, analysis and scho-

Kodály's father was a railway official first in Kecskemét, later in Galánta (Galanta) and Nagyszombat (Trnava). During his grammar school years Kodály studied the piano, violin and cello, and composed a mass, an overture and various chamber works. He went to Pest in 1900, where he studied composition at the Academy of Music and Hungarian and German at the university. Beginning in his student years he entertained a lively interest in folksong, though at first only on the basis of nineteenth century collections. He got to know the phonograph cylinders Béla Vikár had brought back from his collecting tours in Transylvania, which were the first to provide an aural image of living folk-song and reveal the ancient musical

---

larly investigation of Hungarian, Romanian, Slovak, Ukranian, Serbian and later Turkish and Arab folk-music. He began teaching piano at the Academy of Music in 1907, and from 1908 his compositions were regularly published. After 1920 he made many appearances as a pianist in practically every European country. From 1934 he returned to his work as an ethnomusicologist under the auspices of the Hungarian Academy of Sciences, participated in international scholarly activity. Because of the growing pressure of Hitler and fascism he emigrated to the United States in 1940. There he put into notation the recordings of Serbian folk-music at Columbia University, New York. Bartók died in New York in 1945. Most important orchestral works: *Kossuth*–symphonic poem (1905), *Suite No. 1* (1905), *Suite No. 2* (1905–1907), *Two Portraits* (1908), *Two Pictures* (1913), *Four Pieces for Orchestra* (1912), *Dance Suite* (1923), *Piano concertos Nos 1 and 2* (1927, 1930–31), *Music for Strings, Percussion and Celesta* (1936), *Violin Concerto* (1937–38), *Divertimento* (1939), *Concerto* (1942–43), *Piano concerto No. 3* (1945). Stage works: *Bluebeard's Castle* (1911),*The Wooden Prince* (1914–16), *The Miraculous Mandarin* (1918–19). Vocal work: *Three Village Scenes* (1926), *Cantata profana* (1930), *27 Choruses* (1935), *From Olden Times* (1935), many folk-song arrangements. Chamber music: *String Quartets Nos 1-6* (1908, 1915–17, 1927, 1928, 1934, 1939), *Sonatas Nos 1 and 2* for violin and piano (1921, 1922), *Rhapsodies Nos 1 and 2* for violin and piano (1928, 1928), *44 Violin Duos* (1931), *Sonata for Two Pianos and Percussion* (1937), *Contrasts* (1938), *Sonata for Solo Violin* (1944). Outstanding among the large number of piano pieces is the cycle *Mikrokosmos* (1940). Also songs and folk-song arrangements.

layers that lay hidden beneath the more superficial and widespread Hungarian-style popular song (nóta).

By that time Bartók, too, had already encountered Székely (Szekler, i.e. Transylvanian Hungarian) folk-song. Bartók, – the composer reared on German Romanticism – was first inspired to explore national music by the movement of national revival at the beginning of the century and its accompanying wave of anti-Habsburg sentiment. This in fact hardly went beyond the ideals of the nineteenth century, just the emotional verve behind it was greater and more genuine than that of its predecessors, who had been content to seek colourful moods. Bartók's sense of the veracious which accompanied him throughout his life, in which he was unsparing of his own self, did

---

** Zoltán Kodály was born in Kecskemét in 1882. His parents were amateur musicians, the family moving to Galánta (Galanta) in 1884, where they remained until 1892. There the boy became acquainted with instruments, folk-song and instrumental folk music. He began playing instruments and to compose during his grammar school years at Nagyszombat (Trnava). In 1900 he entered Budapest University, specializing in Hungarian and German literature, at the same time studying composition at the Academy of Music. He wrote his university graduation thesis on the strophic structure of folk-song. He began collecting folk-songs in 1905. In 1907 he continued his studies in Paris, and became acquainted with the music of Debussy. At the Academy of Music he taught music theory and composition. His works first appeared in public in 1910. In 1913 he founded, together with Bartók, a project for a new encyclopaedic collection of Hungarian folk-songs. During the revolutionary events of 1918-19 he was deputy director of the Academy of Music, which activity he was later deprived of his post as teacher. The great success of *Psalmus Hungaricus* brought him acknowledgement both in Hungary and abroad. From 1927 he occasionally conducted his own works. From 1925 his attention turned more and more towards musical education and the extension of a more widespread musical culture. His lectures, articles and compositions made him a leading figure in the movement to reform musical education and the rebirth of the choral movement. During the Second World War he gave shelter to many persecuted people, and after the war took an active part in the cultural reconstruction of the country. During the Stalinist years he defended the cause of Hungarian culture combining expediency with firmness and high principles. From 1951 he

not let him rest content with Strauss's influence or the verbunkos inheritance. He first heard Székely folk-songs in 1904, and, picking up the scent, as it were, set out to track it down. He began to transcribe of Vikár's phonograph cylinders. The influence of Kodály, who already in 1905 had begun regular collecting trips in villages, reached Bartók at the best possible moment. It took both of them away from the musician's way of life they had inherited, they wanted to find what was missing in the existing collections: authentic folk-song which would serve them as a compass-guide throughout their lives. In 1907, Bartók went to Transylvania, from where he returned with a great many pentatonic folk-songs, which he was able to compare with Kodály's collection. They shared the field between themselves, and during seven years of intensive collecting work, Kodály went to Upper Hungary, Csík county and Bukovina, while Bartók went to the Székely area and Southern Transdanubia. Bartók also included the minority groups in Hungary in his sphere of interest: Slovak and Romanian folk-music owe their first thorough, scholarly and representative collections to him.

The two musicians set out on this road at the eleventh hour. Although there have been collectors since then who have found new material in some of these regions, still it was the turn of the century that provided the last oppor-

was the head of the Ethnomusicological Section of the Hungarian Academy of Sciences. He died in 1967 in Budapest. His main works are: Stage works: *János Háry* (1925–27), *The Spinning Room* (1924–32). Orchestral works: *Summer Evening* (1906), *Dances of Marosszék* (1923–29), *Dances of Galánta* (1933), *Peacock Variations* (1937–39), *Concerto* (1939–40), *Symphony* (c. 1930–1961). Vocal works: *Psalmus Hungaricus* (1923), *Buda Castle Te Deum* (1936), *Missa brevis* (1944), and many pieces for mixed, male, female and children's choirs. Chamber music and solo works: *String Quartets Nos 1 and 2* (1916–18), *Cello Sonata* (1915), *Seven Piano Pieces* (1910–18), *Serenade* (1919–20). Songs and folk-song arrangements.

tunity of encountering living folklore in its full flowering over large territories. Things which in most areas today exist only as faint memories dating from distant childhood years then formed a living reality complete with its social environment. Naturally, of course, neither then nor perhaps ever at any time folk culture they signify a "pure source" (*Cantata Profana*), as this refreshing stream had often to be cleaned of all kinds of mud by much hard work. Still, what they found was really a source of renewal for both of them. In this respect they remained musicians and composers also in their capacity as scholars. In most places in the Western hemisphere the collection of folk music has become a field for scholars whose sole consideration is to achieve comprehensiveness recording everything with equal importance to obtain accurate knowledge. For them the "people" represents a sociological reality and all the music used by this people is considered as folk music. Bartók and Kodály did not mix scholarly and practical considerations either while setting down the material and their scholarly attitude in notation and classification surpasses even that of their colleagues. But as composers they also sensed something of that scholarly and scientific truth which can be approached only through aesthetic values. Even though it is not easy to define authentic folk music, by contrasting it with late Romanticism and the mannerisms of Hungarian national Romanticism, they did not lose their way when investigating the valuable and the worthless, the old and new phenomena of folk culture, those that belonged to its golden age and those marking its decline.

The influence of folk-music became apparent in the works of the two composers at different times and in different forms. Kodály's first major work (*Summer Evening*) was first performed in 1906. His experience of folk-song surfaced first in arrangements and in songs to popular or classical poems. One can clearly see in his piano music and chamber works how (despite the insertion of some folk tunes and pentatonicism) his individual world of harmony and melody grew, filtered from late Romanticism and, from 1907, showing the influence of Debussy.

In Bartók, too, folk-song first appeared in the form of arrangements (*Three Folk-songs from Csík County, For Children,* etc.), which also sought ways to synthetize traditional harmony with the new melodic material, or in some cases to see whether the melodic discoveries of folk-music could produce new harmony. Overall it is rather the musical trends of the beginning of the century that can be felt–but with a mature, already masterly sense of design, and for splendid orchestration–as seen in great, individual works like the *String Quartet No. 1*, the *Two Portraits* and the *Two Pictures.* In these one still finds the duality characteristic of the educated composers of the end of the nineteenth century: international stylistic features in the large works and Hungarian material (in Bartók's case folk-music) employed in shorter character pieces. The first major synthesis appears in the opera, *Bluebird's Castle* (1911), which virtually compelled the composer to find a synthesis. The text calls for an assimilation of the declamation and motifs of folk-song, while the operatic form prompts a concentrated use of all the musical means he had acquired up to that time.

In 1907, both Bartók and Kodály were appointed teachers at the Academy of Music. Their talent and musical attainments were never questioned even if some of their works, or certain parts of them, were considered strange. They themselves, however, felt that their activity is in connection with public musical life, and neither ethnomusicology nor composition can be carried on in a void. The results of a folk-music research should be incorporated into academic and social public consciousness, while simultaneously the constantly growing void between new music and the art of performance should be removed. This gave rise to a plan for an encyclopaedic collection of Hungarian folk-music, which, according to its first version, was to include the music of the minority ethnic groups in Hungary as well. However, the necessary support for the realization of this project, was not forthcoming and 1914 also put an end to the collecting tours. At the beginning of the second decade of the century, after 1910, there appeared at long last a generation of young instrumentalists who were willing to devote themselves to the cause of new music. Bartók and Kodály attempted to revitalize the concert scene with contemporary music also by founding the Hungarian Society for New Music, and Bartók also by his frequent appearances there as a pianist. In vain however did a younger generation of music critics begin their endeavours (Géza Csáth, Sándor Kovács and Antal Molnár), with growing vehemence official musical circles, audiences and critics rejected music that broke with Romanticism. For Bartók and Kodály the years around 1914 signified the end of a period, forcing them to retire into their studies. This retirement, however, did not remain a barren one, as in both of them it brought to maturity what even then was more than just a bold initiative.

Zoltán Kodály's Educational Project

The works Kodály composed between 1914 and 1918 continue more or less the series of works from the previous years: they consist of chamber music (*String Quartet No. 2*, *Sonata for Cello and Piano*, *Serenade*) and songs. At the same time that these compositions began to assume a more individual character by a more thorough amalgamation of the folk-music element with Kodály's harmonic world, so also there began to proliferate attacks against them. Kodály came to realize that in fact it was not his person, his talent or his style which caused the problem, nor even the resistance always met by innovators. The real obstacle was the general lack of acquaintanceship with folk-song, since "those who enter into the spirit of this music, will understand new Hungarian music much more easily."

In the development of Kodály's educational ideas, the earliest element chronologically was the "resurrection of folk-song". "Folk-song has not yet said its last word: it is not the remnant of an obsolete style and is not one of the lifeless relics of history, it is life itself." This chain of ideas includes two reasons for resurrecting folk-song: its artistic value and its power to express true national unity, a "common spiritual foundation." "Most of the German, French or Slavonic folk-songs do not rise above the aesthetic standard of the charming or naively graceful: they are pretty without any depth. But there are Hungarian melodies which to me and many others signify the same experience as a Beethoven theme." Furthermore: "Hungarian folk-music is not simply the music of the most unrefined and uncultivated class of the population. This music ... was the sole music of the universal nation, of educated and non-educated alike."

Thus the source of a programme of revival springing

from folk-song was rooted in Kodály's personal experience. Tasks were evident in three fields. One, composition in which "our only tradition is folk-style music." Another, to spread folk-song, because if so far the knowledge of the village had salvaged the continuity of tradition, it was now up to the cultivated classes to take it over. "This is how the meadow returns to the nation the treasure that has been faithfully preserved over centuries. It returns it in full, indeed having increased it: its gold scintillates with an antique shine, the fire of its gems has grown deeper. And as the jewel remains a dead treasure at the bottom of the casket and only assumes life when being worn, so too the folk-song grows in its strength to shed light and warmth the more people to whom it belongs." But the condition for getting to know it it is an exact acquaintanceship with it, free of illusion, proceeding along the wearisome stages of collection, notation, analysis and classification, joining the evidence gained from musical history and folk-music.

The next motif appeared late in the 1920s. Kodály felt deeply shocked when he realized that in the rejection of new Hungarian music the two broads layers which otherwise are in opposition to one another took the same stand: musically cultivated people felt the Hungarian character of these pieces to be alien; while the middle classes turned in aversion from the artistic depths of folk-song. This strengthened Kodály's conviction that the condition for the growth of a genuinely Hungarian musical culture was the spread of musical culture as such. The cult of Hungarian music could not isolate the country from general musical culture: "We have belonged to Europe for a thousand years. If we do not want this to be called into doubt. We must embrace all the achievements of the Western European musical tradition."

Kodály considered the choral movement to be the most

important road leading towards this goal. Since "we have to lead the masses to music," it is singing, the instrument which is available to all, and the form of it which creates a community–the choir–that will take us forward if it is used to approach "the invigorating vicinity of the greatest musical geniuses."

Only as a further step did Kodály arrive at the school, which in the years to follow was to take up most of his attention, energy and creative energy. "My attention turned towards the primary school. In the twenties it became clear to me that a musical mass education could only start out from here." But the school had to pave the way, uncompromisingly, for what was the best and the most valuable. "Bad taste scarcely be improved in adults, but good taste developed at an early age is not easily corrupted." This, however, also called for the reestablishment of recognition of the school's role in society and the value of music in the school. It had to be realized that music was "absolutely necessary for man's development ... it is not some superfluous luxury article."

Yet another thesis was called for to visualize the whole set of resources: a correct definition of what music is. The pure musical idea approached by a road leading via an accurate understanding of rhythm, melody and harmony, calls for educational means which do not lead pupils astray. What helps those understand the idiom of music who are unacquainted with it, is not a programme or some extra-musical association, but making it "tangible" and perceptible in its reality. Therefore the key to understanding music is a cultivated ear, the ability to read and write music and other faculties, all demanding much laborious though, at the same time, joyful work. This by the late 1930s led to Kodály's espousal of solmization, and later the significance he attached to in musical education, and finally, resurrecting the medieval school ideal and to the idea of a "specialized elementary school of singing" with daily music lessons in the curriculum.

While the programme became more and more practical and developed its own techniques, it also became expanded by motifs of taste, tradition and intellectual integration, safeguarding the treasure of human and national values jealously guarded. "Bad music undermines faith in moral laws."

Zoltán Kodály the Composer

From the 1920s onwards, Kodály's work as a composer stands in such close relationship to his educational programme that it can almost be taken as the practical illustration of it. The majority of his work from that time onwards are vocal compositions, with pieces written with an educational intent assuming a growing place among them. Folk-music inspiration is not restricted to individual works or certain elements of major works but permeates the fabric of works as a whole. And the Hungarian cultural heritage (literary, historical and musical) is also assigned a growing role within Kodály's scope of preservation and the spreading of his aims.

The long series of folk-song arrangements forms the backbone of Kodály's *oeuvre*: for voice and piano, with elaborate harmonic dress (*Hungarian Folkmusic*–57 ballads and folk-songs), light children's choruses and lengthy choral suites (e.g. *Whitsuntide Procession*, *Songs of Karád*, *Mátra Pictures*). Already in the period after 1910 Kodály felt particularly attracted to the task of composing worthy settings of works of early Hungarian literature. He continued to write song cycles, but now his favoured means of transmitting the words became the choir. The choral piece became Kodály's most expressive genre, in which he used the technical skills and formal possibilities

of composition as an art. Simple choral pieces might became large sets, cantatas constructed on an almost symphonic scale (e.g. *Ode to Ferenc Liszt*, *Jesus and the
Traders*). The range of texts and themes expands and
together with this goes an increase in the overall cultural
message of the pieces, while at the same time the musical
traditions behind the works and the compositional devices
necessary to them become more differentiated. This leads
to an inclusion of the traditions of Catholic and Protestant
church music (*Five Tantum ergo's*, *Advent Song*, *Song to
King Stephen the Saint*, *Balassi's Song of Repentance*,
Geneva psalm arrangements), the traditions of the old
schools so highly esteemed by Kodály (*Horatii carmen*,
Cohors generosa, Hungarian choral pieces in antique
metre), and towards the end of his life, the world of general
European culture (medieval literary texts, Shakespeare,
John Masefield poems, etc.). These works use a highly
varied set of resources. When compared with the concert-
platform works, here Kodály's colourful harmonic world
is pushed slightly into the background, these choral pieces
being dominated rather by the polyphonic element, mostly
drawing their motifs from the used melodies, this also
being true for the harmony employed as well. The frequent
use of short passages of pseudo-imitation lends animation
to the choir and contrasts with the chordal progressions
which bring about a massive choral sound, at the same
time forming a bridge that leads towards Kodály's beloved
sixteenth century choral polyphony. Kodály also makes a
bold use of colouring, and of lively figurative elements of
an almost instrumental effect, often to illustrate the words
or as a means of tone-painting and onomatopoeia. One
always feels that the composer wants to give pleasure to
choristers and listeners alike, sametimes showing a pen-
chant for humorous musical effects.

Psalmus Hungaricus, the work that has remained Kodály's most popular composition, appeared in 1923, foreshadowing in a concise form all the characteristics of the decades to come. *Psalmus* uses no actual folk melodies, but develops both its melodic and rhythmic elements from folk-music, so that it can be considered Kodály's symbol of Hungarian art music built on folk music. The ancient biblical theme, the prophetic tone, the rhythm of the *volta* following the poetry of the sixteenth century poet, Mihály Kecskeméti Vég, all refer to Hungarian historical traditions. The radiant sound of the orchestra and the pathetic tune recall national Romanticism, while other sections join memories of Baroque polyphony to the new musical idiom.

Kodály, Z.: Psalmus Hungaricus, bars 31-38.
The orchestral part is based on the piano reduction: Universal, 1924.

Nagy szük - sé - gem - ben   ne hagyj in - ge- met,

Mert   meg-e - mész - ti   nagy bá - nat szí - ve- met .. .(etc.)

... (etc.)

(I entreat you, my Lord God,
turn your hallowed eyes upon me,
do not abandon me in my dire need,
because the deep sorrow eats away my heart...)

As we have seen in the choral works, from the 1930s
a more generally European tone became stronger in Kodály. Perhaps this was also partly because by that time he
was surrounded by a host of ardent disciples, to whom he
needed to show that the path he represented did not confine
their work to within the borders of Hungary, but rather
served as a link with the wide world. This seems to find
an echo in the Buda Castle Te Deum of 1936, not only in
its choice of text but also its style, a mixture of the sounds
of musical history in general and an individual, Kodályean
sound once again prevailing more strongly.

But Kodály intended folk-songs to reach audiences not
only in choral arrangements. As in the period after 1910

they conquered the concert platform with piano accompaniment, now they invaded the operatic stage. The songs interpolated in *Háry János* (1926) fill the framework of the nineteenth century *népszínmű* (play about peasants using popular art-music) with genuine folk-music material, at the same time embellishing the attractive land of folk-tales with effective interludes. In *The Spinning Room* the song arrangements provide a continuous musical fabric, almost producing the illusion of opera.

It is in *Háry* that Kodály first turns definitely back to the *verbunkos* tradition. Initially, as in the case of Bartók, he felt rather an understandable aversion to the musical material of *verbunkos*. Both composers must have returned to it through the verbunkos elements preserved in instrumental folk-music, but while in Bartók's late verbunkos imitations (*Rhapsodies Nos 1 and 2* for violin, *Contrasts*) its role remained purely musical, Kodály seemed to wish to do justice to this nineteenth century music out of historical and national considerations. Such a twofold, historical and folk-music interpretation informs his two great dance compositions, the romantically glittering folk material set into a long chain in the *Dances of Marosszék* (1930) and the *Dances of Galánta* (1933), scored for full orchestra.

Besides Kodály's ample vocal output there is a strikingly small number of instrumental works from this period. Apart from the two dance suites just mentioned, the orchestral versions of folk-song in the *Peacock Variations* (1937) and *Concerto* (1939) come under this heading. This draws attention to the sacrifice Kodály the composer must have made in the interests of his educational programme. In number and length of works, Kodály cannot be considered a prolific composer. Had he proceeded along the road he embarked on when he wrote promising piano and chamber-music works during a single decade, he certainly would have left behind a richer selection of concert music, but he rather opted to turn his attention and energy to the multi-faceted cause of public musical education. During the last twenty years of his life he devoted practically all his creative energy to writing *bicinia*, short two-part exercises intended for children. Although we find in them the technical assurance and imagination of the learned musician, all is subordinated to educational purposes.

Another sacrifice for Kodály was when he chose texts for the majority of his works which meant they were fully effective only to people who know Hungarian literature, thus depriving them of part of their due recognition. Yet another sacrifice he made is hard to put into words. His interests and attainments led him to concentrate on practical tasks, leaving him little leisure to explore the very newest paths of music, and to fully sample its consequences as a composer. For him his work always served an idea, a mission, and at the end of his life's work one is left with the feeling that Kodály rarely found the time to be alone with music, and his own problems as a creator. Certainly he often had to restrain his imagination to achieve his goal. And so the romantic musical idiom and world of imagination which initially he had imbibed almost instinctively, remained throughout a determining factor and inevitably entered into many various mixtures with the folk material. Although the main reason for his remaining distant from the growing international trend of the mid-century lay in his taste and world of imagination, another reason may have been that his imagination concentrated not so much on the problems of the developing musical idiom, than on the realization of objectives lying beyond this. Kodály was without doubt extremely understanding of mood, character and the specific timbres stemming from "the whole". He could enter into the spirit of the world of the verbunkos just as easily as that of Vivaldi or folk-music. It was not in his make-up to demolish these worlds in order to construct from their elements a newer category unity with an individual synthesis.

· Béla Bartók

Bartók, perhaps even more often and in greater detail than Kodály, wrote about the great opportunity the discovery of Hungarian folk-music provided for the composer. "Every art has the right to be rooted in another, earlier art, and indeed, not only does it have the right to be, it must be so. Why should we then not rightfully assign such a root-bearing role to folk-art as well?" And yet, examining their works, the worlds of Kodály and Bartók are so widely different that one almost doubts the existence of a common basis. If they really developed their styles from folk-song, then why are they so utterly different?

Their difference have both internal and external causes. Included are their differences in make-up as composers and musicians in general, not the least difference being their circumstances, backgrounds and spheres of interest and activity. Bartók's retiring, reserved disposition prevented him from taking any active part in the ground-work of a reform programme. He followed the work of revival with obvious interest and supported it both as a pianist and a composer of educational pieces (or rather, pieces that can be considered educational, e.g. children's choruses, *44 Violin Duos, Mikrokosmos*). But beyond his composing activity, he regarded the systematic and thorough study of folk music as his mission in life. At his own request he was released from teaching in 1934, from that time onwards carrying out his ethnomusicological work at the Academy of Sciences. He notated with minute precision many hundreds of folk-songs, carefully analyzing them, observing every tiny element of their structure, and arranging them in a repeatedly revised overall system. Bartók's opinion was that songs are best catalogued according to a system based on rhythm, and his careful analysis of the basic rhythmic elements of the songs bore also on his outlook as a composer. Bartók's world as a composer is influenced also by the fact that in his scholarly work he gave the same attention to studying Romanian, Slovakian, Arabian, Turkish and Serbian folk-music as to Hungarian. Although his outlook was permeated by the idea of the community and the affinity of the various bodies of folk-music, even so the many different areas of music revealed to him sharpened his analytical sense in determining melodic and rhythmic factors, and prompted the discovery of many new, previously unfamiliar rhythmic formulae, interval combinations and tonal possibilities.

At the same time as he remained in close day-to-day contact through folk-music with such elementary phenomena, his career as a concert pianist confronted him meanwhile with the great styles of European musical history, its great syntheses and standards of art-music. Again, this was not just at the level of distant admiration, experiences in the concert-hall, or music-making for pleasure, he had to wrestle with the material both technically and intellectually, providing the one only version which is created on the concert platform. His wide repertoire embraced Bach, Scarlatti, Mozart and Beethoven as well as Brahms, Liszt, Debussy, Kodály, and of course his own works. His concert activity was unbelievably profuse, in the concert hall and on the radio, and particularly abroad, in Germany, Britain, Switzerland, the Soviet Union and the United States. Bartók was a travelling artist like Liszt, playing with prestigious orchestras, conductors and fellow soloists, sensing the current of the international musical scene, and able ceaselessly to measure his own activities against it.

As he himself said, he always felt happiest in the small

Hungarian villages, among the simple peasants. At the same time, he played music with, and maintained correspondence on an equal footing with, the world's greatest figures. Bartók's extra-compositional activities-between the phonograph and the concert podium–seem to illustrate the synthesis that lies in his work as a composer. While his works, with their relentless precision, perfect construction and explosive force all combined with an elegance, seem to comprise the apparent antithesis of his life.

Descriptive summaries usually discuss Bartók's oeuvre divided into stylistic periods. Thus, the style of the decade from 1910 (roughly from *Bluebird's Castle* to *The Miraculous Mandarin*, or rather to the first and second Sonata for Violin and Piano /1921–22/) was marked by an increasingly deliberate departure from Romanticism together with a parallel contrast between on the one hand a strong, closed manner of construction, apparent in the direct or indirect adaptations first of Hungarian, and then of Slovakian, Romanian and Arabian folk-music, and on the other an expansive manner of composition in the "free" works, extensive and responding to every effect. It was at this period that Bartók came closest to Schoenberg's innovations, even if from an independent route, and precisely therefor was able to preserve the results of this exploration into his later years.

The same period included the score of the *Wooden Prince* (1914–16), a gem of Bartók's enchantingly fresh world of fairyland and nature, and the *String Quartet No. 2* (1916–17), whose outer movements still refer back to the harmonic world of the first quartet, but whose middle movement already anticipates the stricter manner of construction of the following period. The second ballet, the *Miraculous Mandarin* (1918–19), to a libretto by Menyhért Lengyel, which at the time seemed very bold, giving rise to much indignation, and which has since suffered

from many symbolic interpretations, not only has music
fall of rich, multi-coloured portrayal but also abounds in
devices for unification which increase the organic character of the work, and which began to appear ever more
consistently in Bartók's later works, the background of the
composition relying on a delicate ear and hard intellect.
The continuitiy and naturalness of the changes in the music
are brought about the birth of new structural elements in
a section which is at the same time giving full display of
its own energies. The conscious alternation of motives and
interval structures, repeating them and deriving them from
one another, all this–together with other composing processes– represents such a comprehensiveness and unified
sanity of composition that straightaway it ranks the composer, still in his thirties, among the greatest names.

That this was a fertile decade for Bartók is borne out
by many piano works (e.g. *the Suite op. 14*, *Colindas*, *Fifteen Hungarian Peasant Songs*, *Etudes*, *Improvisations*)
and songs. His arrangements now showed absolutely clearly that his direct and profound knowledge of folk-song
deriving from his research work, instead of making him
adhere rigorously to *cantus firmus*, led him rather take out
those characteristics of the song in question that coincided
with the demands of his own work, and deal with them in
ways suited to his own problems as a composer. Thus from
being 'arrangements' the works turn into independent
compositions, the borderline slowly disappearing between
the sovereign treatment of a folk-song and an individual
piece amalgamating into its own style the creative elements of folk-song. The finest example of this process is
Improvisations, a Bartók work fully individual in sound,
form and treatment of the piano. Folk-song still functions
as a guideline, it ensures a sense of tonality in what is
otherwise a newly acquired dodecaphonic language stabi-
lizing basic intervals in the interests of a tonal arrange-

ment, and the outlines of a verse structure counterbalance the web of continuous transitions, motivic development and contrapuntal whirls, at the same time articulating the overall form.

A great work of synthesis: the *Dance Suite* (1923), with its mature construction and youthful verve marks a borderline between two periods. It is usually regarded as a summing up resulting from the study of various bodies of folk-music, documenting a kind of international esteem for folk-music. But a more thorough analysis shows that, even with all its surface variety, it is perhaps the first Bartók work which has a thoroughgoing uniformity. A path leads within and through the five movements, without any break. The now sifted out basic formulae expand like an avalanche, creating internal tensions only to turn them into the music's prime mover. Eventually everything which at first seemed contradictory becomes unified in the greater system newly brought about. The ritornello is not the only, nor the principal thing that holds this lengthy work together, but rather this formity, the homogeneity of a fashioning imagination and in the higher sense of the term, technique.

The *Dance Suite* was followed by three years of silence, which precede the next, classical period. After 1926, the structural unity of Bartók's works becomes even stronger, the development of tonality more consistent and stricter. The sign of a strengthening Baroque influence is the all-pervading contrapuntal technique, the more consistent motivic structure replacing broadly arched melodic phrases. There is also some "false" development. The pieces of this period appear more daring, more "barbarous", more dissonant, there is more kinetic rhythm, chords dashed off in masses, note clusters falling like blows. This, however, is only the semblance. The kinetic movement is only unbroken to the extent that it is in a Baroque concerto. In reality a sensitive articulation carves the uniform fabric into precise rhythmic formulae which are put to varied use during the construction. The massed chords signify not so much a more homophonic and less articulated thinking as a more profound contrapuntal thinking, affording concerning points of encounter between simultaneous sound processes. Even less than in the previous period can one speak of accidental note combinations done for effect. Every note is set in a precisely measured network of relationships, measuredness ruled by an intellectually controlled but uniquely delicate ear. The "dissonances" are mainly the product of an increased aural capacity, the result of hearing the tonal system as one, and of a carefully arranged cumulation of simultaneous processes.

It would be mistaken to divide the works of this period into two groups according to whether one sees them as the Bartókian equivalent of a Neo-Classical/Neo-Baroque European trend, or as rather the continuation of the folk-music influence. Folk-song, even in the arrangements, provides only a single strand in the formal and tonal process outlined above, while the most abstract works always assume their marked, clearly outlined, naturally flowing quality under the effect of a motivic development, a use of intervals and a rhythmic articulation found in folk music.

The period begins with a few piano pieces which show Bartók's "new" means of composition, in practically their most radical form: *Out-of-doors* (1926), *Nine Little Piano Pieces* (1926), the second and third pieces of *Three Rondos* (1927), and particularly the monumental *Piano Sonata* (1926). It seems that this change matured first in the workshop of Bartók the pianist, which then gave renewed meaning to the classical form cycles in the *Piano Concertos Nos 1 and 2* (1926, 1931) and the *String Quartets Nos 3 and 4* (1927, 1928). The heightened role of the wind and percussion in the piano concertos and the percussion-like style of the piano parts help realize a more objective, non-romantic sound ideal. This however is also closely linked to the full development of Bartók's formative processes: a more well-defined motivic configuration takes the place of dissolving musical phrases. In the quartets, Bartók uses the strings in the same way. The process of structuring is the same regardless of whether the superimposition of the motifs and the sound relationships they incorporate are expressed polyphonically in the traditional sense of the term, or in a stratification of specific timbres and performance techniques.

A comparison of this manner of composition with great music of the period in other countries leads us to use the paradoxical term "static dynamism". Unfolding, development, a logical progression, are undoubtedly a part of the classical and romantic inheritance of Bartók. (A logical continuation, in its own manner, of this tradition was the direction associated with the name of Schoenberg.) But in Bartók this development is achieved not by an unbounded flood, but in strictly measured stages, with practically the calm of a mathematical operation. It remains stationary, exactly clarifying its position without being swept away by the impetus of the form. But this articulation, this division into small steps is not the same for instance, as Stravinsky's mosaic technique. Even though in the end this formal instinct is the secret of Bartók's genius, we are perhaps justified in also hearing in it things peculiar to the history of Central European, and particularly Hungarian music. A symbol of this paradoxical stationary and yet progressive way of formation and also a means of expressing it, is the symmetrical "bridge form" (ABCBA i.e. palindrome form). In it every return, or rather back reference, is infused with the memory and effect of sections heard since its first appearance.

Cantata Profana, completed by 1930, shows evidence of this complex inheritance, both in itself and in its programmatic origin. The text comes from a Romanian *colinda* (Romanian Christmas carol) in Bartók's translation, about the desire for triumphal revival through nature– something which in this form, could only be brought about in Eastern Central Europe. At the same time, it unites musically the most modern idiom with the legacy of the Baroque oratorio.

Folk-music arrangements are of course not absent from this period either. That these arrangements clearly stem from Bartók's creative imagination and not just from folksong is shown by the fact that they conform stylistically with the "free" works dating from the same period. Because of this, one of Bartók's most gripping *original* works is the *Twenty Hungarian Folk-songs* (for voice and piano, 1929), using the idiom of folk-song but expressing the composer's own highly individual voice. Beside them we can list the *Rhapsodies Nos 1 and 2* which create a large form out of folk-music material (for violin and piano, 1928), as well as the choral sets of *Hungarian Folk-songs* (1930) and *Székely Songs* (1932).

This period also saw the composition of *Mikrokosmos* (153 piano pieces from the earliest stages to concert pieces, 1926–1939), *44 Violin Duos* (1931) and *27 Unmixed Choruses* (1935). These are Bartók's contribution to the new Hungarian educational endeavours, showing at the same time how the content of great works can be transferred to smaller dimensions, with restrictions of both sound and form. But the new Hungarian choral movement was assisted by Bartók not only in its early stages, but also with a great work, one might say a choral sonata (*From Olden Times*, for male voice choir, 1934) in which he also showed to what heights this genre can rise. Composed to folk texts the work points the attention of the choral scene, subordinated to educational goals, to the purely musical value of the *a cappella* style, and its significance directed beyond practical goals, as had earlier been the case in polyphonic choral music and Bach's motets.

The period ends with the most representative works of Bartók's *oeuvre*. The pliant, multi-coloured musical material and instrumentation of *String Quartet No. 5* (1934) approximates most closely to the world of Mozart's string quartets. *The Sonatas for Two Pianos and Percussion* (1937) is more playful, relaxed and joyful than Bartók's earlier works, even in its fairly robust sections. Finally these few fruitful years, spent in the hard daily work of folk-music research, concert tours in Hungary and abroad, weekly radio recordings, plus the composition of some two or three great works a year–this last period also yielded Bartók's most effective work, *Music for Strings, Percussion and Celesta* (1936). This is the work studied by young musicians and analysed by musicologists in their efforts to uncover the secrets of Bartók's art. It is listened to again and again by the music-lover who wants to encounter, in a single work, Bartók's full significance. The great fugue of the first movement is not only a revival of Bach, but summary of the very essence of the tonal development of ten centuries. The second movement shows that the classical sonata has not lost its message in the twentieth century, at the same time finally harmonizing the closed formal world of folk-music with the large forms of art music. The third movement is usually said to incorporate the Hungarian lament into art music. At the same time, it also shows that a European rationality, foresight and planned character do not stand in opposition to the depths of artistic experience and sensitivity. The fourth movement, usually ranked among the great Eastern European round dance finales, is also one of the most detailed and abstract Bartókian formal conceptions.

Bartók, B.: Music for Strings, Percussion and Celesta,
first movement.

The *Violin Concerto* (1937–38) happily combines a style bordering on the dodecaphonic with quite loosely structural forms, its broad melodic language and almost romantic tone already signifying a transition. The output of the last decade of Bartók's life–a decade overshadowed by tragic historical developments, personal problems, departure from his native country, the cares of the American years and approaching death–is usually regarded as a kind of quietening down, a reversion, a period of reconciliation condemned by avant-garde musicians and praised by the conservative. The familiar forms and intonations of classicism, the cantabile melodic language, the larger role assigned to triads, the restricted use of "dissonances" all seem to confirm this view. The lyricism of *String Quartet No 6* (1939) is only overshadowed by a fleeting attention to the grotesque sounds of Mars, and the ease of the *Divertimento* (1939) only in passing by the wail of the second movement. Even the heroic character of the sonata movement of the *Concerto* (1943), the tone of its scherzo, the chorale reminiscences and its teeming finale seem like a concession to audiences reared on the Romantic symphony, just as the *Piano Concerto No. 3* (1945) does to the Apollonian ideal of the piano concerto. Even so, this is not a question of an about-face, but rather a new conquest, a logical continuation, the crowning of an *oeuvre*.

For a division into periods only serves to apportion Bartók's works from a particular stand-point, and to express the first, surface impressions made by the works. A deeper analysis reveals that Bartók's oeuvre is characterized, over several decades by a one-way development, and even a basically identical approach to composition. We have, in fact, no right to speak of Bartók's different styles, as it is one and the same individual synthesis that marks the elements seemingly applied in so many differing proportions.

For Bartók, folk-song, the same as dodecaphonic arrangement of notes or the classical tradition, serves as the starting point for an analytical process. In those works which do not contain any folk-song arrangement, he breaks down the folk-music styles into their smallest elements, after arriving at their fundamental interval relations and rhythmic formulae, uses them to construct the organic development of a compositional idea. This view of Bartók undoubtedly puts him apart from those Western European developments which practically dissolved the tonal sense of this expanded tonal structure. So be enriched the fabric of interval structures, mirror formulae, etc. with the assertion of new factor. In doing this he did not follow a completely individual and arbitrary course, but simply drew the conclusion always inherent in European musical development, a conclusion which before then had not been revealed. His synthesis resolves the duality between folk-song arrangement and free composition: folk-song is present in the free compositions in the form of an elemental idiom, while each arrangement realizes an individual compositional idea.

At the same time this Bartókian structure is not simply a rigid system to be filled subsequently, as it were, by musical contents treated instinctively and dictated by moods and emotions. Only in the greatest masters in musical history have musical-emotional content and structure appeared in such organic unity.

This synthesis has an immense capacity to imbibe. Since great unity and an individual compositional approach always leave their features imprinted on the musical material, its elements can more daringly take on new musical influences without becoming eclectic. This is why the last period is only an apparent revision and quietening down. Bartók did not return so composing in the major and minor. As earlier, too, he always handled folk-song by fitting it into his own, tonally organized, dodecaphonic ear, so that triads were also given a Bartókian character in the fabric of the composition. They preserve that same mastery of the musical *punctualism* discernible in the works dating from the 1920s: a Bartókian principle by which each note is responsible to itself, entering as a single note into a relationship with other single notes. Viewed like this, the last works can even be considered Bartók's boldest, as they explore the extent to which his style has become strong enough to interpret even the most traditional element within its framework. Bartók's works always maintain their own independent organization and meaning they are organisms which construct and indicate their own microcosms.

In Bartók the history of Hungarian music in preceding centuries reached in a certain sense its goal: the world of folk-song, the modality and European character of the Middle Ages, the technical accomplishment of the German school, the desire of the nineteenth century to create art music that was Hungarian in character but of world significance. But Bartók is also one of the possible summaries of the development of European music history as well. In Bartók Hungary addressed the world for the first time in a way that made Europe listen. There is probably nothing else in Hungarian history that could be added so directly and absolutely to the great intellectual treasury of mankind. Thus Bartók's significance has proved to reach beyond music. His life's work, his artistic morality, his commitment and universality have worked to help heal a nation's wounded self-respect, at the same time serving as a standard for all men's achievements in all fields.

Musical Life between the Two World Wars

The most original initiative in the field of music between the two wars was the great educational programme initiated by Kodály, which was intended to put the master's ideas into practice in three related fields: singing instruction in schools, the choral movement, and church music. The main aims were musical training based on folk-song, the dissemination of modern Hungarian music, the removal of the second-rate "music" widely used, and the carefully planned introduction of European masterpieces in teaching of singing. The movement, which took its name from the periodical *Magyar Kórus* (Hungarian choral music) in the spirit of Kodály did not approach the gifted few, but wished to reform the people as a whole, not just in a musical sense. It therefore naturally turned almost exclusively to vocal music. Only after 1945, during the course of the reorganization of music schools, did progressive music teachers apply these principles to instrumental teaching as well, including wide layers of amateurs instead of solely concentrating on professional training, and replacing the use of primitive etudes for beginners with the performance of folk-songs, shifting the emphasis from technical considerations to musicality. The Magyar Kórus movement had a profound effect with is outstanding educational and organizing methods and after some initial opposition, it was joined and supported by a great many teachers and church musicians. In spite of its shortcomings (such as the cult of teaching pieces under the pretext of spreading new Hungarian music, scant connections with the "large" musical scene, and, related to this, the danger of becoming amateur in character), the movement was one of the purest, most sweeping and promising development in the modern history of Hungarian music until it was baned after the Second World War.

⟂ The mutual distrust between the camp of Kodály supporters, who practically formed a party, and the professional musicians, once again divided the Hungarian musical scene, which was all the more harmful for both sides because the time was just ripe for the higher echelons of musical life to harvest the benefits of the previous fifty years. These showed themselves in the high standard of Hungarian musicians touring or emigrating abroad, such as violinists (e.g. Ede Zathureczky), pianists (e.g. Ernő Dohnányi, Béla Böszörményi Nagy, György Faragó, Géza Anda, Andor Földes), singers (e.g. Anna Németh, Endre Kóréh), and conductors (e.g. György Solti, Jenő Ormándy, György Széll) plus the growing number of orchestras in Budapest and in the country towns (e.g. the Royal City Orchestra, now the State Concert Orchestra). These all marked the achievements of a long, constructive period.

Hungarian musicology and musical criticism came of age between the two wars. Practically all the important fields found their scholars (musical psychology: Géza Révész, music history: Kálmán Isoz, Ottó Gombosi, Ervin Major, etc., theory and aesthetics: Géza Molnár, Aladár Tóth, Antal Molnár, scholarly music pedagogy: Sándor Kovács), and in the person of Bence Szabolcsi there appeared a personality who had a sound grip of the separate fields and was able to link them together, combining philological and musical approaches with the ability to reach a synthesis. He even fulfilled Kodály's premises in a synoptic treatment of the history of music and folk-music research. Successors to the great pioneers also appeared in ethnomusicology, continuing first of all the work of collection (László Lajtha, Pál Péter Domokos, György Kerényi, Lajos Kiss, Pál Járdányi and Lajos Vargyas). The most notable achievement in the field of folk-music collection was the series of records issued under the *Patria* label, which presented a selection of folk material performed by the best folk singers, and has remained ever since the gold standard of folk-music archives.

Well edited periodicals also gave witness to a growing intensity in musicological work, with special journals covering practically all the fields (scholarly musical review, education, general knowledge, the youth movement).

The Musical Scene after 1945

After 1945 (or rather 1948), the new government undertook the running and maintaining of this whole system of musical functions, essentially eliminating private activities and those of small communities. They declared that the inherited "progressive" tradition must serve the welfare of the whole people and accordingly, urged that general school and music school education be extended, that the doors of the opera house and the concert halls be opened wide, and that provincial musical life be developed. Musical institutions were incorporated into a centralized system and new institutions were set up in fields where they had not existed. The National Music School was raised to an intermediary educational level (called a "conservatory"), similar institutions were set up in the provinces, and a uniform network of schools was brought about, consisting of general music schools, medium-level conservatories, and the Academy of Music (with lower-grade teachers' training colleges attached to it). Simultaneously the material of singing instruction in schools was reworked according to Kodály's principles, and, later, elementary schools with daily singing lessons (not yet with a professional character) were also introduced.

The process of unification included concert promotion (with the State Philharmonia, as the central concert agency), music publishing, orchestra management, and the professional union of musicians.

Musicology was assigned premises in the form of the Bartók Archives and the Folk-Music Research Group, and later the Institute for Musicology, which united the two, as well as the Musical Archives of the National Széchényi Library, and the music department of the Ethnographical Museum. This soon led to the launching of major projects, representative publications and extensive specialized studies contributing to their work. A great host of professional and volunteer collectors helped toward the publication of the series *Magyar Népzene Tára* (Corpus Musicae Popularis Hungaricae–an anthology of Hungarian folk-music), launched in 1951 (with seven volumes having appeared so far). There also began the publications of the surviving melodies of early Hungarian music history (*Collection of Old Hungarian Melodies* I-II), the publication of Bartók documents and the study of material in musical archives (e.g. the Haydn manuscripts in the Esterházy estate). The experienced senior scholars (Bence Szabolcsi, Dénes Bartha, Benjamin Rajeczky, Lajos Vargyas, Kálmán Csomasz Tóth, Géza Papp) found well-grounded assistants in the musicological department of the Academy of Music, established by Kodály and Szabolcsi, who by the 1960s and '70s were producing prominent scholars of international renown (including László Somfai, György Kroó, János Maróthy, Bálint Sárosi, László Vikár and Janka Szendrei).

This musical policy, however, with its mixture of good intentions, propaganda, and narrow-minded party views, did as much harm as good to musical culture. The strict, dictatorial leadership, centralization leading to hegemony, and a mode of government subordinating everything to political ends, paralyzed social forces and produced a damaging one-sidedness.

With this came the fear produced by the power of personal and clique cults wearing the disguise of an ideological approach, and a too comfortable attitude resting on ready-made forms.

It was composition that faced the gravest situation. The biennial "plenary meetings" were veritable martial law courts instead of festivals of creative power. In this period Bartók was ostracized as cosmopolitan and pessimistic, while the works of Stravinsky, Schoenberg and other leading twentieth century composers were similarly banished from the concert hall for ten years.

The cultural policies gave rise to many forms of musical popularization and the many programme-notes for concerts, popular courses, sales of cheap records and tickets, a massively subsidized choral movement and professional educational literature, though of good service for the cause of music, could not avoid the effects of overregulation, the prevalence of a political slant, and being diluted for the sake of popularity. (The choral repertoire, for instance, was crammed with political songs instead of masterpieces, while a superficial cult of folk-song prevailed alongside the ideological support of conservative taste.)

Amateur forms of music-making, like chamber-music clubs, music-lovers' societies, activities initiated by citizens, fell victim to this centralization. And of course it was impossible for church choirs both as regards the choir members and the faithful to fulfil their cultural role.

In the field of music too, personality cults grew up and multiplied the web of authority with its mutual support basis, inevitably producing a selection of the unfittest, the results of which lasted for several decades. Added to this was the large wave of emigration in 1956 and the slack attitude produced by the lack of any competition, all of which meant that Hungarian performing standards were in a disastrous state by the 1970s.

All these developments are to be seen in the field of composition as well.

Composition

The effect of Bartók, and particularly of Kodály on Hungarian composition was actually felt only from the 1930s onwards. Until then, and concurrently even afterwards, many composers continued to work under the banner of late Romanticism, at most enriching their music with a superficial folk-style tint. Ernő Dohnányi and Albert Siklós (1878–1942) worked in the spirit of German Romanticism, and Leó Weiner (1885–1960), who was widely esteemed for his great professional knowledge and his activities in musical education, persisted in this style the longest (divertimentos, suites, incidental stage music, and string quartets).

László Lajtha (1892–1963) composed under the spell of the French music of the beginning of the century. His rich output (nine symphonies, an opera, ballets, ten string quartets, chamber music, masses, and choral works) reflects his encounter with folk-music. He was the first composer to be associated with the work of folk-music collecting, though his technique, with its colourful harmony and its counterpoint links him to foreign models. Another foreign model determined the work of Sándor Jemnitz (1890–1963), who imitated and championed the style of Schoenberg.

The overwhelming majority of composers who began their careers in the 1930s, made their debuts as pupils, or at least as followers, of Kodály, which together with personal and conceptual ties, determined their principles, aims and styles as composers as well. The composers most directly conditioned by Kodály's example, including Lajos Bárdos (1899–1986), served the choral movement and the schools with their untiring educational and organizational work, and with arrangements which are easy on the ear and easy to teach.

The late 1920s saw the appearance of Ferenc Farkas (b. 1905), outstanding in his refined taste and great proficiency, Ferenc Szabó (1902–1969), more sensitive to twentieth century chromatic expression, and who as a member of the Communist Party left for the Soviet Union, but returned to Hungary in 1945 to acquire leading positions there, and Pál Kadosa (1903–1983), who in his compositions incorporated wide experience gained abroad and a stylistic knowledge more extensive than the Hungarian average (in this standing closer to Bartók and the new Western European schools of composition). Sándor Veress (b. 1907), who embarked on his career in 1931, can also be ranked among the members of this generation. Veress studied composition with Kodály, and clearly followed his example by becoming the most fertile cultivator of teaching literature during the following fifteen years, as a composer translating Kodály's ideas into instrumental instruction as well (piano pieces, light chamber music, choral pieces). His strict manner of construction, contrapuntal skill and a feeling for large forms raised him above his contemporaries as one of the most distinguished members of the second generation. In this he shows the Bartók inheritance just as he does in his openness towards foreign influence. After leaving Hungary (in 1948), he managed to fit into the European musical scene and include neoclassical, later dodecaphonic, features in his style without upsetting the essential Hungarian balance of his music.

From the second half of the 1930s, this generation of composers was joined by a slightly younger generation, who used the new Hungarian idiom with ease, but as a result produced a rather unsophisticated style (János Viski 1906–1961, Endre Szervánszky 1911–1977, Pál Járdányi 1920–1966, György Ránki 1907–1991). Their facile, pentatonic textures, learned yet somewhat stereotyped use of form, was actually the requisite for starting a career, so it

is not clear what direction they would have taken person-
ally, dependent upon talent and reflection, if external circumstances not exercised an influence on them stronger
than was necessary.

After the Soviet "Zhdanovean turn", the style of composition in Hungary, too, became a political issue. "So-
cialist realism", requiring clarity, popularity, an optimistic
and heroic form of expression, and for the most part a
progressive subject for it programmatic "lesson" also–this
at a time when Bartók and contemporary music from
abroad were banned–joined with Kodály's idiom to create
a new Academicism. Thus the typical genres of the 1950s
were hackneyed folk-song arrangements free of problems,
strident choral songs, serenades, divertimentos, concertos
redolent of cloudless happiness, programme symphonies
with a militant and victorious tone, heroic stage works imitating romantic grand opera and musical comedies tending
towards operetta. The pentatonic language in use for two
decades, modal harmonization, and Romantically inspired
colouring chords now became the obligatory hallmarks of
an ideologically backed style. Even so, despite these restrictions, audiences encountered a few works which rose
considerably above the monotony of the "courtly style"
due to the composer's creative talent, faith in his attempt,
and occasional risk-taking in pursuit of truth (e.g. the concertos by Viski, Járdányi's *Vörösmarty Symphony*, Szervánszky's *Concerto*, Ferenc Szabó's *In Fury Rose the
Ocean* and Rezső Sugár's *Heroic Song*.)

The reshaping of society and culture that began after
1956, brought a sharp change in composition. Even be-
forehand there had been indications. First the excommuni-
cated figure of Bartók, deemed unfit for emulation, surfaced as a model for young composers still in their student
years, who now dared to show his "formalist" legacy in
their own works. This following of Bartók was textbook,

unorganic and epigonal, restricted to a few chords, melodic sections, contrapuntal processes and rhythmic diminutions which at the time were daring. As well as this of course imitting characteristic Bartók moods was at the time a clandestine delight, but it all served to help liberate a generation of composers.

The next influence was the idiom of dodecaphony, heard about mainly by reputation, or possibly recordings. The unsettling of the tonal framework until then regarded as immovable, the transformation of the composer's methods, thinking in terms of tonal structures rather than musical moods, the possibility of experimenting with music– all this had a profound effect on the 25-30-year-old composers, added to which was the catalytic effect of the Polish school and the reports brought home by a few composers traveling abroad.

The first work showing clearly the commencement of a new period did not come from the younger generation: it was Endre Szervánszky's *Six Orchestral Pieces,* premiered in 1960. But it offered a new lease of life for the generation who attended the Academy of Music in the 1950s who welcomed these new musical opportunities, just as their teachers had welcomed the modern Hungarian music of the 1920s. Of course the first etudes written in the fervour of discovery, or dodecaphonic features mixed into a style merely marked the breaking open of locked doors. It was not, in fact, a question of transplanting the Viennese school to Hungary, the 1960s produced works which rather instinctively sought to join together the contemporary trends they had got to know and the musical achievements of some three-four decades in Hungary which, willy-nilly, had become a tradition. Now composers were much more individual, using different nuances and procedures than composers had in the previous decade. Common to them all however, is the inclusion of dodecaphonic features in their style after a certain filtering, with a moderating, dampening instinct inherent in Hungarian taste. Even if in altered circumstances, Bartók's formal ideal, his motivic fabric and rhythm and his compositional programme thinking in terms of development and diminution, still prevails also in those pieces oriented towards the West. This led to the development of a particular "Hungarian eclecticism" (as György Kroó puts it) whose tonal organization is nourished more by the Viennese approach to sound–by now virtually a universal style–but whose melodic and formal elements reach back, through secret channels, to Bartók.

It proved to be useful to Hungarian music that the norms of the dodecaphonic schools were not applied in a rigid, mechanical way. For in the following years the tyranny of a technique for some time believed to be the only true one, everywhere started to loosen, giving way rather to pluralistic paths of composition. Harbingers of this new mentality were György Kurtág (b. 1926), András Szőllősy (b. 1921) and Rudolf Maros (1917–1982) from the previous generation, together with a new generation that started out in the 1960s and '70s. However to review and evaluate the works by this group of composers working with a knowledge of the whole arsenal of contemporary music is no longer the task of the musical historian but of the musical critic. And as we do not wish to be unjust by singling out a few names, we shall simply point out the role of the New Music Studio, formed in the 1970s. On the one hand this was intended to provide a performing background for contemporary music for which there had been a long-felt need, and on the other it was to educate audiences for a new music which turns away from heated emotional effects, preferring contemplation and working with a differentiated use of small devices.

Mention should be made of Hungarian composition be-

yond the country's borders, composers living in the territories annexed to neighbouring countries and those living
in emigration, since they, too, are a part of Hungarian
musical culture, having been reared on it and having
enriched it.

Musicians and audiences in Hungary obtain hardly any
news of the work of composers in neighbouring countries.
A few names from Yugoslavia, Slovakia and the Carpathian Ukraine, and a slightly longer list of name and works
from Romania–this is all that penetrate the cultural borders. The historical development that have occurred in
Hungary can be sensed, even if slightly delayed, in
Transylvania. Thus a somewhat conservative, late-Roman-
tic composition style (Géza Kozma, b. 1902, Vilmos De-
mián, b. 1910, Gábor Jodál b. 1913, and Albert Márkos
1914–1981) was followed, from 1944 onwards, by the appearance of a generation with a more individual colouring,
reflecting a three-fold influence. Firstly, a consciousness
of their folk-music and Hungarian music-history inheritance (in which strong emphasis is also given to a special
Transylvanian tradition, revealed particularly by the activity of János Jagamas, Zoltán Kallós, András Benkő and
Ferenc László). Another influence is evidence of contact
with Romanian musical culture, particularly folk-music,
and the third is an opening up towards new stylistic tendencies together with the far from easy task of amalgamating them with traditions (e.g. in the works of Tibor Oláh,
b. 1928, among the elderly, and Boldizsár Csíky, Csaba
Szabó and Ede Terényi among the younger composers).

As in the case of performers, many composers too have
left Hungary in recurring waves, seeking new homes
abroad. The number of those emigrating during the first
half of the century (Ödön Pártos 1907–1977, Mátyás
Seiber 1905–1960, Tibor Serly 1901–1978, Jenő Takács
b. 1902) and leaving the country after 1945 (Ernő Dohná-

nyi, Sándor Veress) grew further after 1956 (György Ligeti, Iván Erőd, later Péter Eötvös). A larger proportion of their music is naturally taken up by the tradition or topicality of their new environment, but all of them have preserved the marks of their Hungarian upbringing, either directly (evident in their compositional material) or indirectly (appearing in their use of form).

The last 10-15 years cannot yet form the subject of a musical history. We close this outline therefore with a few brief comments.

The gradual lifting of restrictions in the previous years means there are no longer any obstacles of principle for Hungarian composers, and musicians in general, preventing them from joining their activity to the musical culture of the rest of the world. Many Hungarian composers have been given the opportunity of having their works performed in concert halls and on the radio abroad, while many Hungarian performers have made guest appearances or spent several years with foreign musical companies and orchestras. The meagre flow in the opposite direction is due only to financial difficulties: performances of new works in Hungary are delayed or even postponed (which is something the annual two-week festival *Music of Our Time* can hardly remedy), and noted foreign performers and ensembles rarely appear on the Hungarian concert platform. This, however, would be much to be desired for several reasons. Standards of measurement could be of a stimulating effect on Hungarian instrumental, and above all, orchestral culture in its present state, and at the same time might help lure (or lure back) audiences into concert hall.

Abroad, attention to Hungary's musical life as been aroused mainly by Kodály's musical education project. This is justly the case, as it combines a purposeful educational approach, based on humanistic European traditions, with a successful technique. But while hundreds of visiting teachers, after attending courses in Hungary, take home these ideas to introduce them into their own education systems, in Hungary there are not unjustified fears whether the deterioration of the personal, conceptual, methodical and organizational conditions of singing and musical education can be checked.

The institutions of musical life have also suffered from the economic difficulties of the 1980s These have affected, for instance, support for musicology. Nevertheless, in all probability it is not this but personal reasons that have cause a decrease in productivity, a slackening of a previous dynamic development, and a certain barrenness of ideas and dejection in folk-music research, as well as in the field of musical historiography.

A welcome development in the concert scene is the forging ahead of the provinces (forming orchestras and organizing festivals) the appearance of ensembles playing early music (even if with varying standards) young performers learning to play new music, and the appearance of ensembles. Low public interest in contemporary music is, of course, not confined to Hungary. Even so, an overall decrease in interest in music in Hungary may also have played a part. This is not just the result of the forging ahead of commercialized light music and the consequent loss of a new audience of young people: it can be explained by the vogue for in-de-siecle behaviour patterns, mostly imported from America and Western Europe, bringing aggressiveness and hedonism–in part appearing as a counter-effect to the previous repression–and the general crisis of intellectual values, of appreciating culture and the European inheritance of humanism. And this is the point where Hungarian music now shares the problems of the world of culture in general.

Appendix

Selected Bibliography and Discography

CHM   Centuries of Hungarian Music (A magyar zene évszázadai) ed. Bence Szabolcsi, in Hungarian

CMPH   Corpus Musicae Popularis Hungaricae

COHM   Collection of Old Hungarian Melodies (Régi Magyar Dallamok Tára) ed. Kálmán Csomasz Tóth and Géza Papp, in Hungarian

HMHS   Hungarian Music History Studies (Magyar Zenetörténeti Tanulmányok), in Hungarian

MD   Musicological Dissertations (Zenetudományi Dolgozatok), in Hungarian

MS   Musicological Studies (Zenetudományi Tanulmányok), in Hungarian

StM   Studia Musicologica (in non-Hungarian languages)

The following list is intended for the general reader who may wish to read further on various subjects or to listen to recordings. It makes no claim to be a classified bibliography for scholarly research. Books are given with their full titles, articles for brevity's sake mostly feature with the author's name, and the date and page number of the relevant periodical. Publications in foreign languages are marked by obelisks. The discography carries records on the Hungaroton label.

Summaries of General Hungarian Music History SZABOLCSI, B.: *A Concise History of Hungarian Music* (Budapest, 1964). The Hungarian original (*A magyar zenetörténet kézikönyve*, 3rd revised and enlarged edition Budapest, 1979) offers the most extensive number of music examples available. For more de-

tailed descriptions of the periods see: SZABOLCSI, B.: A magyar
zene évszázadai I-II (Budapest, 1959, 1961–Centuries of Hungarian Music, henceforth CHM), and also see: KODÁLY, Z.-BAR-
THA, D.: Die Ungarische Musik (Leipzig, 1943). DOBSZAY, L.:
Magyar zenetörténet (Budapest, 1984–Hungarian Music History). A rich collection of documents, complete with short introductions and notes is provided in LEGÁNY, D.: A magyar zene
krónikája (Chronicle of Hungarian Music, Budapest, 1962). An
annotated picture album: KERESZTURY, D.-VÉCSEY, J.-FALVY, Z.:
A magyar zenetörténet képeskönyve (Picture Book of the History
of Hungarian Music, Budapest, 1960). An extensive selection
of principally monophonic material (folk-songs and art-music
examples): DOBSZAY, L.: A Magyar Dal Könyve (Book of Hungarian Song, Budapest, 1984). Musicalia Danubiana a series of
music from Hungarian sources, launched a few years ago
(material from the Middle Ages to the late eighteenth century,
with introductions in several languages, 12 volumes so far, see
below).
For brief material on composers see: SZABOLCSI, B.-TÓTH, A.-
BARTHA, D.: Zenei Lexikon (Musical Encyclopaedia, I-III, Budapest, 1965). Partial studies have appeared in the series of
books and periodicals: Zenetudományi Tanulmányok (Musicological Studies, henceforth MS), Magyar Zenetörténeti Tanulmányok (Hungarian Music History Studies, henceforth HMHS),
Studia Musicologica (henceforth StM) and Zenetudományi Dolgozatok (Musicological Dissertations, henceforth MD). An anthology of Hungarian music history on records (partly only arrangements MUSICA HUNGARICA (SLPX 12143-7). Selection of old
Hungarian music: MAGYAR UDVAROK ZENÉJE XIII-XVIII. SZÁZAD
(Hungarian Court Music, 13th-18th Centuries, SLPX 11491-3).

Chapter 1 For a summary description of Hungarian folk-music
mainly from a formal point of view see: BARTÓK, B.: A magyar
népdal (Budapest, 1924, in English: The Hungarian Folk-Song,
ed. B.Suchoff, Albany, 1981), the same with a historical evalu-
ation: KODÁLY, Z.: A magyar népzene (Budapest, 1937/1973, in
English: Folk-Music of Hungary, Budapest 1971). Recent summaries: VARGYAS, M.: A magyarság népzenéje (Hungarian Folk-

Music, Budapest, 1981), *A magyar népdaltípusok katalógusa* (Vol. I, Budapest 1988, in English: *The Catalogue of the Hungarian Folk-Song Types*, Budapest, 1992). Essay towards a summary of the history of folk-music before the establishment of the Hungarian Kingdom: VARGYAS, L.: StM 20 [+3]-73. Representative editions of folk-music material: collection of music examples in Bartók's work quoted above, the collection of examples edited by L. Vargyas in Kodály's book quoted above; JÁRDÁNYI, P.: *Magyar népdaltípusok* I-II (Hungarian Folk-Song Types I-II, Budapest, 1961) and the series by LAJTHA, L. (*Népzenei monográfiák* - Folk-Music Monographs). *A magyar népzene Tára* (*Corpus Musicae Popularis Hungaricae* - Anthology of Hungarian Folk-Music): music examples of children's games in Vol. I, of laments in Vol. V, of the fifth-shift in style in volumes VI-VII, and of custom songs in Volumes II and III. On diatonic laments: VARGYAS, L.: MS 1953: 611-57, DOBSZAY, L.: *A sirató-stílus népzenénkben és zenetörténetünkben* (Lament Style in Hungarian Folk-Music and Music History, Budapest, 1983), in a shorter version, in English: Dobszay, L.: StM 15: [+]15-78. On the pentatonic ("psalmody" lament style: DOBSZAY, L.–SZENDREI, J.: *"'Szivárvány havasán'. A magyar népzene régi rétegének harmadik stíluscsoportja"* ("'A Rosemary Bush..' The Third Stylistic Group of the Old Layer of Hungarian Folk-Music") in *Népzene és zenetörténet* III (Folk-Music and Music History III, Budapest, 1977, 5-101). On the fifth-shifting style see Vargyas's study quoted already and the introduction to Vol. VI of *Corpus Musicae Popularis Hungaricae* (henceforth CMPH). On the problem of the style's Finno-Ugrian affinity: VIKÁR, L.: *"A magyar népzene volgai török és finnugor kapcsolatai"* ("The Volga Turkic and Finno-Ugrian Relations of Hungarian Folk Music") in *Magyar őstörténeti tanulmányok* (Hungarian Prehistoric Studies), Budapest, 1977, 291-304.

Discography Hungarian folk-music material arranged largely according to style: HUNGARIAN FOLK-MUSIC (LPX 1187) and HUNGARIAN FOLK-MUSIC I-II-III (LPX 1800-04, 10095-8, 18050-53). A representative selection of the material recorded and notated by Bartók, naturally without stylistic considerations: LPX 18069 and 18058-60. From Kodály's collections: LPX 18075-76.

Chapter 2 Besides the general literature listed in the introduction (which was still based on scanty information regarding the Middle Ages), an up-to-date summary–including all the themes to follow–with a full bibliography: *Magyarország zenetörténete I. Középkor* (The History of Hungarian Music I. Middle Ages), ed. RAJECZKY, B., Budapest, 1988 (English translation in preparation). For the 'Symphonia Ungarorum' BALOGH, J.: *Szent Gellért és a 'Symphonia Ungarorum'* (St Gerald and the 'Symphonia Ungarorum'), Budapest, 1926, and GÁBRY, Gy.: StM 12: [+]291-7. On the position of music in medieval Hungarian culture and education MEZEY, L.: *Deákság és Európa* (Classical Culture and Europe), Budapest, 1979: on liturgical choirs relations briefly, *idem*: *Acta Litteraria*, 1968: [+]29-46. Detailed information on the musical life in schools and churches in BÉKEFI, R.: *A népoktatás története Magyarországon* (The History of Public Education in Hungary), Budapest, 1906, and *idem*: *A káptalani iskolák története Ma-gyarországon 1540-ig* (The History of Chapter Schools in Hungary up till 1540), Budapest, 1910. On liturgical customs in Hungary, in connection with the tabular depiction of a section: DOBSZAY, L.–PRÓSZÉKY, G.: *Corpus Antiphonalium Officii–Ecclesiarum Centralis Europae. A Preliminary Report*, Budapest, 1988. A summary picture of Gregorian practice in Hungary can be found in Vol. I of *The History of Hungarian Music* and DOBSZAY, L.: Plainchant in medieval Hungary: *Journal of the Plainsong and Mediaeval Music Society* 13 (1990): 49-78. Material publication: Rajeczky, B.: *Melodiarium Hungariae Medii Aevi I* and *Supplement* (melodies of hymns and sequences), Budapest, 1981, 1982, and SZENDREI, J.–DOBSZAY, L.–RAJECZKY, B.: *Cantus Gregorianus ex Hungaria* (selection of choirs), Budapest, 1981. Text edition of the Offices of Hungarian saints: DANKÓ, J.: *Vetus Hymnarium Ecclesiasticum Hungariae*, Budapest, 1893, music edition: FALVY, Z.: *Drei Reimoffizien aus Ungarn,* Budapest, 1968, cf. MEZEY, L. in *Magyar Századok* (Hungarian Centuries), Budapest, 1948, 41-51, FALVY, Z.: StM 6: [+]207-69. On the history of Hungarian notation: facsimile edition of the *Codex Albensis* with an introduction: Falvy, Z.-Mezey, L.: *Codex Albensis. Ein Antiphonar aus dem 12. Jahrhundert*, Budapest-Graz, 1963.

SZENDREI, J.: *Középkori hangjegyírások Magyarországon: I. A magyar notáció története, II. Német neumaírások Magyarországon* (Medieval Score Notations in Hungary. I. The History of Hungarian Notation, II. German Neume Notations in Hungary: 133 facsimiles, with a summary in German), Budapest, 1983, and *idem*: StM 27: ⁺139-70, and 28: ⁺303-19, and *Magyar zene* (Hungarian Music), 1978: 130-43. A summary and catalogue of medieval Hungarian notated sources, with 107 facsimiles: SZENDREI, J.: A *magyar középkor hangjegyes forrásai* (Notated sources from the Hungarian Middle Ages, with a German summary), Budapest, 1981. On minstrels: SZABOLCSI, B. in: *Gedenkschrift für Hermann Abert*, Halle, 1928: ⁺154-64, Pais, D.: MS 1953: 95-110, FALVY, Z.: StM L: ⁺29-64. On troubadours: Eckhardt, S. in *Irodalomtörténeti Közlemények* (Proceedings on Literary History) 1961, 129-37, FALVY, Z.: in *Magyar zene* (Hungarian Music) 1974: 44-50 and StM 15: ⁺79-88. Many data concerning secular music-making set in a colourful picture of medieval culture: ZOLNAY, L.: A magyar muzsika régi századai (Bygone Centuries of Hungarian Music), Budapest, 1977. On folk-music remains traced back to the time of the House of Árpád: SZENDREI, J. in *Magyarország Zenetörténete I* (The History of Hungarian Music I), on recitative tradition in folk music, idem: StM 13: ⁺275-88, in greater detail, with many music examples in: *Népzene és Zenetörténet III* (Folk Music and Music History III), Budapest, 1977, 65-123, on *regölés*: PAIS, D.: in *Magyar Századok* (Hungarian Centuries), Budapest 1948, 5-23, KERÉNYI, Gy.: StM 3: ⁺181-214, SZENDREI, J.: *Bulletin de l'Institut de Musique, Académie Bulgare des Sciences*, 1969, ⁺341-50, StM 9: ⁺33-53, StM 16: ⁺133-50.

Discography A fairly rich selection of the Gregorian repertoire in Hungary: GREGORIAN CHANTS FROM HUNGARY (SCHOLA HUNGARICA): I. Christmas (LPX 11477), II. Advent, Whitsun (SLPX 12048), III. Holy Week (SLPX 12049), Easter (SLPX 12050), Hungarian Saints (SLPX 12169), Blessed Virgin Songs, Funeral (SLPX 12170), using mainly material from Hungarian codices: *The Memory of Thomas Becket* (SLPD 12458), *The Book of Wisdom* (SLPD 12534), *Easter's Herald* (SLPD 12558), *Epiphany* (SLPD 12559), *Gergorian Chants in a Village Church* (SLPD

12742), *Hungarian sacra* (SLPX 31044), *From Night to Night* (SLPD 31085). On secular music: *Peire Vidal–A Troubadour in Hungary* (SLPX 12102).

Chapter 3 Regarding the material treated in this chapter, both a summary and a detailed picture, with data and a bibliography, can be found in Vol. I of *The History of Hungarian Music*. For some subjects information can be gathered from the works listed in the previous chapter, as far as the late Middle Ages. For musical life in churches and schools, *see* the works by BÉKEFI, R. and MEZEY, L. already quoted. For organs, other instruments and for instrumentalists: SZIGETI, K.: *Magyar Zene* (Hungarian Music), 1947, 186-201 and 1975: 380-88. ZOLNAY, L.: StM 14: +385-400, 16: +151-78, and idem: in *Folk Music and Music History*, Budapest, 1974, 125-48. For Bálint Bakfark *see* complete edition of his works: *Opera omnia* I-III, Budapest, 1976, ed. Homolya, I. and Benkő. D. *See* also: HOMOLYA, I.: *Bakfark*, Budapest, 1982. For the musical scene at Buda Castle: KUBINYI, A.: StM 9: +77-97, StM 15: +89-100 and *Magyar Zene* (Hungarian Music) 1975, 389-92, ZOLNAY, L.: StM 9: +99-113, MOÓR, E.: in *Ungarische Jahrbücher* 1937: +57-86, GOMBOSI, O.: in *Muzsika* (Music),1929: +27-39, and in REESE, G.: *Music in the Renaissance*, London, 1954. +714-27, HARASZTI, E.: in *Mátyás Emlékkönyv* (Memorial Volume in Honour of King Matthias), 1940, II. 289-412, Corvina 1940: +35-52, Corvina 1940: +760-73, and in JAACQUOT, J.: *La musique instrumentale de la renaissance*, Paris, 1955, +35-9, SZIGETI, K.: in *Magyar Zene* (Hungarian Music), 1968, 402-28. For polyphony: SZIGETI, K.: StM 6: +147-68, and in *Musica Antiqua Europae Orientalis–Acta Scientifica Congressus*, Bydgoszcz, 1966, +223-26, Brewer, Ch.E.: StM 24: +5-19, SZENDREI, J.: MD 1982: 19-38. For the structure of Gregorian traditions in Hungary: DOBSZAY, L.: StM 27: +37-65, *cf.* Ullmann, P.: StM 27: +185-92. For fourteenth and fifteenth century sources, *see* Szendrei, J.'s catalogue mentioned in Chapter 2, and SZIGETI, K.: StM 4: +129-72. SZENDREI, J.-RYBARIC, R.: *Missale Notatum Strigoniense ante 1341 in Posonio*, annotated facsimile edition (*Musicalia Danubiana*, 1, Budapest, 1982. For the late layer of Gregorian chant, besides information in *The history of Hungarian Music*, *see*: RAJECZKY, B.: StM 19: [+]227-34. For notation see the bibliography for Chapter 2. For the edition of László Szalkai's textbook: BARTHA, D.: *Das Musiklehrbuch einer ungarischen Klosterschule in der Handschrift von Fürstprimas Szalkai 1490.*, Budapest, 1934. For recent research which has ascertained that Szalkai was the student of a municipal school: MÉSZÁROS, I.: *A Szalkai-kódex és a XV. század végi sárospataki iskola*, (The Szalkai Codex and the Sárospatak School in the Late Fifteenth Century) Budapest, 1972. For the musical notation of the notes: SZENDREI, J.: in *Magyar Zene* (Hungarian Music), 1984, 185-93. For the "Old Hungarian Lament of the Virgin Mary": SZABOLCSI, B.: in *Vers és dallam* (Poetry and Melody), Budapest, 1959, 33-49, but cf. with my comments in Vol. I of *The History of Hungarian Music*, MEZEY, L.: in *Acta Litteraria*, 1969, [+]21-28, and also DOBSZAY, L.: in MD 1988. For the Te Deum in the *Peer Codex*: Szendrei, J.: StM 14: [+]169-201 and 15: [+]303-20. An up-to-date summary of popular hymns sung in the vernacular features only in Vol. I of *The History of Hungarian Music*, but *cf.* PAPP, G.: *A magyar katolikus egyházi népének kezdetei* (Beginnings of the Hungarian Catholic folk hymns), Budapest, 1942, and on some of the examples: Dobszay, L.: StM 13: [+]203-13 and *Acta Ethnographica*, 1971, [+]387-410. On the epic song: DOBSZAY, L.: MD 1982: 39-55. On the ballad: Vargyas, L.: *Hungarian Ballads and the European Ballad Tradition*, Budapest, 1983. Summary of folk-songs and folk customs of medieval origin in Vol. I of *The History of Hungarian Music*, for the various melodic types: *The Catalogue of the Hungarian Folksong Types* I (mainly in Chapter III). For vagante songs: SZABOLCSI, B.: MS 1953: 743-51, for the melodic family illustrated by the last music example in the present chapter: SZENDREI, J.: in *Ethnographia*, 1973, 737-443.

Discography Medieval Gregorian and polyphonic chants on the *Schola Hungarica* records mentioned under the previous chapter (particularly GREGORIAN CHANTS FROM HUNGARY I, II, IV and V). On the music of the royal court, with selections from works of foreign composers at the court: MUSIC AT KING MATTHIAS'S COURT (SLPX 11844), MUSIC IN BUDA CASTLE 1490–1526 (SLPX

11983-4), GEMS OF RENAISSANCE MUSIC (SLPX 11720). COLLECTED
LUTE WORKS BY BÁLINT BAKFARK (SLPX 11549, 11817, 11893,
11988, 11987), lute music including works with Hungarian relations SLPX 11721. The Old Hungarian Lament of the Virgin Mary
in Latin: HUNGARIAN LITERARY REMAINS (SLPX 19172), in Hungarian: HUNGARIA SACRA (SLPX 31044).

Chapter 4 A summary with full bibliography: *The History of
Hungarian Music II* (ed. Bárdos, K.). Besides the bibliography
listed in the introduction, a summary picture of the musical life
of the Transylvanian court and residences: SZABOLCSI, B.: "A
XVII. század magyar főúri zenéje" (Hungarian Aristocratic
Music in the Seventeenth Century) in CHM I, 211-80, and BAR-
THA, D.: *Erdély zenetörténete* (The History of Music in Transylvania), Budapest, 1936. For Diruta: FALVY, Z.: StM 11: [+]123-31.
For the volume of polyphonic vespers of Pozsony, with a complete list of incipits: FERENCZI, I.: StM 17: [+]59-165. For Bártfa
and the Bártfa collection: GOMBOSI, O. in *Festschrift Johannes
Wolf*, Berlin, 1919, [+]38-47, and in *Ungarische Jahrbücher* 1932,
[+]331-40. For the musical scene in Northern Hungary *see* the
introduction to the Zarewutius edition listed below. For the following composers *see* the studies included in the editions of
their work: RAUCH, A.: *Musicalisches Stammbüchlein 1627–
Musicalia Danubiana 2*, Budapest, 1983, ed. SAS, Á., JANCSO-
VICS, A., BÁRDOS, K., FERENCZI, I. and MOLLAY, K., CAPRICOR-
NUS, S.: *Opus Musicum I-II*, ed. Rybaric, R., Bratislava, 1975
and 1979. ZAREWUTIUS, Z.: Magnificats and Motets–Musicalia
Danubiana 8, ed. MURÁNYI, R.Á. and FERENCZI, I. SCHIM-
BRACZKY, J.: *Opera omnia*, ed. Rybaric, R., Bratislava, 1982.
Marckfelner, S.: *Tabulaturbuch*, ed. Matus, Fr., Bratislava, 1981.
REILICH, G.: *Geistlich-Musikalischer Blum- und Rosen-Wald*,
ed. Türk, H.P., Bucharest, 1984. For Daniel Corner *see* POR-
FEYTE, A.: *Musica Antiqua, Acta Scientifica, Congressus*, Byd-
goszcz 1972: [+]551-88, and PERNYE, A.-BENKŐ, D: StM 19:
[+]297-324. For János Kájoni: DOMOKOS, P.P.: "... édes Hazámnak
akartam szolgálni..." *("... I Wanted to Serve My Dear
Country...") Budapest, 1979 (including the full text of the Kájoni
Cantionale),* SEPRŐDI, J. in *Akadémiai Értesítô* (Transactions of

the Academy), 1909, IX/2, 61-70, on the Kájoni Codex, Papp, G. in *Magyar Zenei Szemle* (Hungarian Music Review) II/5, on Kájoni's organ tablature. A publication of sixteenth-seventeenth century monophonic remains (though omitting some of the genres): Csomasz Tóth, K.: *Régi Magyar Dallamok Tára* (Collection of Old Hungarian Melodies, henceforth COHM), I. *A XVI. század magyar dallamai* (Sixteenth Century Hungarian Melodies), Budapest 1958, and PAPP, G.: COHM, II. *A XVII. század énekelt dallamai* (Seventeenth Century Vocal Melodies), Budapest, 1970, both with thorough studies. A collection and historical interpretation of what remains of these melodies in folk tradition: SZENDREI, J.–DOBSZAY, L.–RAJECZKY, B.: *XVI-XVII. századi dallamaink a népi emlékezetben I-II* (Sixteenth–Seventeenth Century Hungarian Melodies Living in Folk Memory, I-II), Budapest, 1979. For verse-chronicles: SZABOLCSI, B.: "A XVI. század magyar históriás zenéje" ("Hungarian Epic Music in the Sixteenth Century") in CHM I: 132-56, SZABOLCSI, B.: "Tinódi zenéje" ("Tinódi's Music) in CHM I: 41-100, also see notes in COHM I. For Protestant graduals *see* the introduction by Ferenczi, I. to the edition of the *Eperjes Gradual* in *Musicalia Danubiana* 9, Budapest, 1988, CSOMASZ TÓTH, K.–BÁRDOS, K. MS VI: 165-264, in Folk Music and Music History, III, Budapest, 1977, 134-256. BÁRDOS, K.: *Volksmusikartige Varierungstechnik in den ungarischen Passionen 15. bis 18. Jahrhundert*, Budapest, 1975, and BÁRDOS, K.: StM 4: +289-396, Ferenczi, I. in Magyar Zene (Hungarian Music) 1982, 49-69. For the history of metrical songs, in minute detail (including the publication Honterus's examples): CSOMASZ TÓTH, K.: *A humanista metrikus dallamok Magyarországon* (Humanistic Metrical Melodies in Hungary), Budapest, 1967, and HONTERUS: *Odae cum harmoniis* 1548, ed. Nussbacher, G. and Philippi, A., Bucharest, 1983. For community singing, alongside the publications quoted already: CSOMASZ TÓTH, K.: *A református gyülekezeti éneklés* (Calvinist Communal Singing), Budapest, 1950, and MS 1953: 287-330, HUSZÁR, GÁL: *A keresztyéni gyülekezetben való isteni dicséretek és imádságok* (Divine Hymns and Prayers in the Christian Community), Komjáti, 1574 (facsimile edition: Budapest, 1986). For the stylistic change in the seventeenth century: SZABOLCSI, B.: "A XVII. század magyar világi dallamai" ("Seventeenth Century Hungarian Secular Melodies") in CHM I: 283-372, also on single melodies: SZENDREI, J.–DOBSZAY, L.–RAJECZKY, B., op. cit. For Baroque melodies: DOBSZAY, L.: StM 16: +15-23. *Tabulatura Vietoris saeculi XVII, Musicalia Danubiana 5,* ed. Ferenczi, I and Hulková, M. Bratislava, 1986. For contemporaneous dance music: SZABOLCSI, B.: A XVI. század magyar tánczenéje" ("Sixteenth Century Hungarian Dance Music") in CHM I: 159-208, and idem: 'A XVII. század magyar világi dallamai" ("Seventeenth Century Hungarian Secular Melodies) in CHM I: 283-372. For the scope of folk-music melodies quoted in the chapter: The Catalogue of the Hungarian Folk-Song Types II (under publication) and DOMOKOS, M.: StM 22: +69-86.

Discography Related to the musical life in Transylvania: MOSTO: GYULAFEHÉRVÁR MADRIGALS (SLPX 11867), DIRUTA: IL TRANSILVANO (SLPX 12108), CRONER: TABLATURE (SLPX 11820-21). Selections form the polyphonic vespers of Pozsony: POLYPHONIC VESPERS FRO CHRISTMAS AND EASTER (SLPD 12533), FROM THE BÁRTFA COLLECTION (SLPX 11669-70). Verse chronicles (in unauthentic arrangements): SLPX 11868. Adapted examples from the material of the Geneva psalms: SLPX 11973. From Protestant melodies: SONGS OF THE HUNGARIAN REFORMATION (SLPX 12665). From dance and song collections: CHOREARUM COLLECTANEA (LPX 11498), SONGS AND DANCES FROM THE VIETORIS MANUSCRIPT (LPX 11577.78), with more remote Hungarian connections: Speer: MUSIKALISCH-TÜRKISCHER EULENSPIEGEL (LPX 11521)

Chapter 5 For the activity of Pál Esterházy and the musical scene at the Esterházy residence: TANK, U.: *Studien zur Esterházysche Hofmusik von etwa 1620 bis 1790,* Regensburg, 1981, DOMOKOS, M.: StM 10: +129-51, and the introduction by Sas, Á. to the new edition of ESTERHÁZY, P.: *Harmonia caelestis–Musicalia Danubiana 10,* Budapest 1989. For Haydn's activity see BARTHA, D.–SOMFAI L.: *Haydn als Opernkapellmeister,* Budapest, 1960, and Vol. VIII of MS (devoted to Haydn). Basic source material on the musical life in towns, churches and

schools in the monographs by BÁRDOS, K: *Pécs zenéje a XVIII.
században* (Music in Pécs in the Eighteenth Century), Budapest,
1976, *Gyôr zenéje a XVII-XVIII. században* (Music in Gyôr in
the Seventeenth and Eighteenth Centuries). Budapest, 1980, *A
tatai Esterházyak zenéje 1827–1846* (The Music of the Esterházy Family of Tata 1827–1846), Budapest, 1978, *Sopron zenéje
a 17-18. században* (Music in Sopron in the Seventeenth and
Eighteenth Centuries), Budapest, 1980, *Eger zenéje 1687–1887*
(The Music of Eger, 1687–1887), Budapest, 1987. Also for the
musical life of towns and the activity of tower musicians, *see*
further studies by BÁRDOS, K.: MD 1983: 103-8, 1684: 13-16,
1985: 13-82, 1986: 45-50. For the musical history of Pozsony
(Bratislava): NOVÁCEK, Z.: *Hudba v Bratislava* (in four languages), Bratislava, 1978. A rich collection of documents from
the period: LEGÁNY, D.: *Chronicle of Hungarian Music*, Budapest, 1962. On this subject see also: SZIGETI, K.: "A szombathelyi egyházmegye egyházi zenéjének története" ("History of
the church Music of the Szombathely Diocese") in *A 200 éves
szombathelyi egyházmegye története* (The History of 200 Year
old Szombathely Diocese), Szombathely, 197, ISOZ, K.: *Buda
és Pest zenei művelődése 1686–1873* (Musical Cultivation in
Buda and Pest 1686–1873), Budapest, 1926. A short summary
about schools by BÁRDOS, K. in *Magyar Zene* (Hungarian
Music), 1981, 5-9. On monastic music: SZIGETI, K.: *Magyar
Zene* (Hungarian Music), 1978, 282-97. Studies of the lives and
works of individual composers have began recently, *see* introductions to the following publications: ISTVÁNFFY, BENEDEK:
Church Music Works, ed. Vavrinecz, V. and Dobszay, L. (*Musicalia Danubiana 3*), Budapest, 1984, BENGRAF, J.: *Six Quartets*,
ed. Sas, Á. (*Musicalia Danubiana 6*), Budapest, 1986, DRU-
SCHETZKY, G.: *Partitas for Wind*, ed. SOMORJAY, D: (*Musicalia
Danubiana 4*), Budapest, 1985, VALENTIN DEPPISCH (1746–
1782): *Te Deum, Magnificat, Vesperae de Confessore*, ed. Sas,
Á. (*Musicalia Danubiana 11*), Budapest, 1990. Edition of eighteenth century monophonic melodies: BARTHA, D.: *A XVIII. század dallamai* (Eighteenth Century Melodies), Budapest, 1935,
an analysis of these: SZABOLCSI, B.: "A XVIII. század magyar
kollégiumi zenéje" (Music in Eighteenth Century Hungarian

Colleges") in CHM II: 4-120. For the musical scene in colleges and the work of György Maróthi: Csomasz Tóth, K.: _Maróthi György_, Budapest, 1978. an annotated edition of Pálóczi Horváth's collection of songs: PÁLÓCZI HORVÁTH, Á: _Ötödfélszáz énekek_ (Four and a Half Hundred Songs), ed. Bartha, D. and Kiss, J., Budapest, 1953. Contemporary dance music: DOMOKOS, P.P.: _Hangszeres magyar tánczene a XVIII. században_ (Instrumental Hungarian Dance Music in the Eighteenth Century, with further bibliography), Budapest, 1978. A basic publication on the origins of the verbunkos, with an introductory study: _Hungarian Dances 1784–1810_, ed. Papp, G., (_Musicalia Danubiana 7_), Budapest, 1986, analyses by Papp, G.: StM 21: $^{+}$151-217, 24: $^{+}$35-97,, 26: $^{+}$59-132, on various collections: DOMOKOS, M.: StM 17: $^{+}$215-47, BÓNIS, F. StM 2: $^{+}$9-23, Kodály, Z. in _Új zenei Szemle_ (New Music Review), 1952, III/6, 1-5, Falvy, Z. StM 13: $^{+}$15-59. On the _verbunkos_ style and the role of gypsy musicians: SÁROS, B. Gipsy Music, Budapest, 1978.

Discography The full material of _Harmonia caelestis_ by PÁL ESTERHÁZY (SLPX 11433-5). Information on the styles of composers active in Hungary in sleeve-notes to records of ALBRECHTS-BERGER (LPX 11349, SLPX 1154), DITTERSDORF (SLPX 11745-6), MICHAEL HAYDN (LPX 1264, 11531, SLPX 11358, 11462, 11530, 11678) and HUMMEL (SLPX 11459, 12014). On HUNGARIAN composers: ISTVÁNFFY, BENEDEK: MUSICA SACRA (SLPD 127733). A work by Druschetzky in a miscellaneous recording (SLPD 12874). For school songs: COLLEGE MUSIC IN HUNGARY (SLPX 11760). For dance music see the material listed for the previous chapter.

Chapter 6 Besides the general bibliography given in the introduction, a basic summary study is: SZABOLCSI, B.: "A XIX. század magyar romantikus zenéje" ("Nineteenth Century Hungarian Romantic Music"), in CHM II: 151-308. Ample documentary material in LEGÁNY, D. _op. cit._ For the choral movement: LEGÁNY, D. in _Magyar Zene_ (Hungarian Music), 1981, 392-422, 1982, 102-11,. For Mihály Mosonyi: BÓNIS, F.: _Mosonyi Mihály_, Budapest, 1960, and _idem_: StM 2: $^{+}$139-87. Summary works on Erkel: LÁSZLÓ, Zs.: _Erkel Ferenc élete képekben_ (The Life of Ferenc Erkel in Pictures), Budapest, 1958, LEGÁNY,

D.: *Erkel Ferenc művei és korabeli történetük* (The Works of Ferenc Erkel and their Contemporaneous History). Budapest, 1958, LEGÁNY, D.: *Erkel Ferenc*, Gyula, 1960, NÉMETH, A.: *Erkel*, Budapest, 1979. *See* also the Erkel volume of 1968 of MS, and BÓNIS, F.: StM 1: +475-85, StM 11: +69-89, StM 13: +321-31, MARÓTHY, J.: StM 1: +161-74. From the vast number of works on Liszt *see*: SZABOLCSI, B.: *Liszt Ferenc estéje* (The Twilight of Ferenc Liszt), Budapest, 1956, GÁRDONYI, Z.: *Liszt Ferenc magyar stílusa* (Ferenc Liszt's Hungarian Style), Budapest, 1936, *cf. idem*: StM 5: +77-87, BÁRDOS, L.: *Liszt Ferenc, a jövő zenésze* (Ferenc Liszt, the Musician of the Future), Budapest, 1976, LÁSZLÓ, ZS.–MÁTÉKA, B.: *Liszt Ferenc élete képekben és dokumentumokban* (The Life of Ferenc Liszt in Pictures and Documents), Budapest, 1978, NÁDOR, T.: *Liszt Ferenc életének krónikája* (Chronicle of the Life of Ferenc Liszt), Budapest, 1975, LEGÁNY, D.: *Liszt Ferenc Magyarországon 1869– 1873*, Budapest, 1976, English edition: Liszt and His Country, Corvina, 1983, HAMBURGER, K.: *Liszt Ferenc*, Budapest, 1980, English edition: Franz Liszt, Corvina, 1987, StM 28: Liszt Volume, and MS 3, Liszt-Bartók Volume. A collection of pseudo folk-art songs of the nineteenth century: KERÉNYI, Gy.: *Népies dalok* (Popular Art Songs, in German: *Volkstümliche Lieder*), Budapest, 196. An excellent analysis of these songs in SÁROSI, B.: *Gipsy Music*, Budapest, 1978. See also: KERÉNYI, Gy.: *Szentirmay Elemér és a magyar népzene* (Elemér Szentirmay and Hungarian Folk-Music), Budapest, 1966. For the new style of Hungarian folk-music from a historical approach: Szabolcsi, B. in *Népzene és történelem* (Folk Music and History), Budapest, 1954, 25-58, a summary of research up till now. VARGYAS, L.: *A magyarság népzenéje* (Hungarian Folk-music), Budapest, 1981, 333-42. The connections with other changes in village life: HOFER, T.: in *Magyar Zene* (Hungarian Musica), 1981, 70-75.

Discography Works by Erkel and Liszt are available in the largest number, including Erkel: HUNYADI LÁSZLÓ (SLPX 1040-2), and BÁNK BÁN (LPX 11376, 11378, SLPX 11535). Of the countless works by Liszt on the Hungaroton label, we mention here his piano pieces with Hungarian connections (LPX 11340, 11488-90,

12203, SLPX 11976-7, 12239), the *Rhapsodies* arranged for orchestra by Doppler (SLPX 11341, 12062, 12249), the organ works (SLPX 11540-44), chamber works (SLPX 11798), and the series entitled *Choral Works*. Works by other composers: Csermák, A.: SIX HUNGARIAN DANCES AND IMPENDING DANGER (SLPX 11698), Mosonyi: PIANO CONCERTO (LPX 1083), GOLDMARK: VIOLIN CONCERTO (SLPX 12007) and his opera, THE QUEEN OF SHEBA (SLPX 12179-82). A clear survey of the turn of the century and the first half of the twentieth century is provided by the memorial disc: A HUNDRED YEARS OF THE ACADEMY OF MUSIC (LPX 11579). Mention should be made also of the label on which Ernő Dohnányi plays his own piano works (LPX 12085-86).

Chapter 7 Practically all the valuable works of the present century are available in score and on record. With the body of relevant writing being so huge, here we can only refer to a few works. On Zoltán Kodály *see*: EÖSZE L.: *Kodály Zoltán*, Budapest 1961, *Kodály Zoltán életének krónikája* (Chronicle of the Life of Zoltán Kodály), Budapest, 1977, and *Kodály Zoltán élete képekben* (The Life of Zoltán Kodály in Pictures), Budapest, 1971, BREUER, J.: Kodály-kalauz (in English: *A Guide to Kodály*, Budapest, 1990), *Kodály-mérleg '82* (A Balance of Kodály '82), ed. Breuer, J., Budapest, 1982, a collection of studies published in memory of Zoltán Kodály in HMHS, 1977, and the Kodály volume of *Studia Musicologica*: StM 25.The collected writings of Kodály were published in the two volumes of *Visszatekintés* (Retrospection), ed. Bónis, F., Budapest, 1974, with a selection of them in English: *The Selected Writings of Zoltán Kodály*, Budapest, 1974. On Béla Bartók: SZABOLCSI, B.–BÓNIS, F.: *Bartók élete képekben és dokumentumokban* (The Life of Bartók in Pictures and Documents, in English, German and French), Budapest, 1964 an 1972. KROÓ, GY.: *Bartók-kalauz*, Budapest, 1970 (in English: *A Guide to Bartók*, 1974), UJFALUSSY, J.: *Bartók Béla* (with discography), Budapest, 1976, and *idem*: *Bartók-breviárium* (Bartók Breviary), Budapest, 1980. TALLIÁN, T.: *Bartók Béla*, Budapest, 1981, English edition: Béla Bartók, Corvina (1988) , LÁSZLÓ, F.: *Bartók Béla. Tanulmányok és Tanúságok* (Béla Bartók. Studies and Evidence), Bucharest, 1980, and *Bartók dolgozatok* (Dissertations on Bartók), Bucharest, 1974, 1976, 1982. SOMFAI, L.: *18 Bartók-tanulmány* (Eighteen Bartók Studies), Budapest, 1982, see also also the studies in Volumes 2 and 10 of MS, Vol. 3 of HMHS and Vol. V of StM. *The Collected Writings of Béla Bartók* was edited by Szöllôsy, A., Budapest 1967, and a selection of his writings appeared in English, entitled *Essays*, ed. B. Suchoff, London, 1976.

On contemporary composers (with a retrospective view over the past decades): KROÓ, Gy.: *A magyar zeneszerzés 30 éve* (Thirty Years of Hungarian Composition), Budapest, 1975. Clear portrayals of the years after 1945 are provided by MARÓTHY, J.: *Zene, forradalom, szocializmus. Szabó Ferenc útja* (Music, Revolution, Socialism. The Path of Ferenc Szabó), Budapest, 1975, BREUER, J.: *Harminc év magyar zenekultúrája* (Hungarian Musical Culture of Thirty Years), Budapest, 1975, and TOKAJI, A.: *Mozgalom és hivatal* (Movements and Ministries) Budapest, 1983.

Discography Of the vast number of recordings of works by contemporary Hungarian composers we shall just point out two classical series in which Bartók plays the piano, performing, among other pieces, works by himself and by Kodály: BARTÓK AT THE PIANO (LPX 12326-33) and BARTÓK RECORD ARCHIVES (LPX 12334-38).

Index

Names of kings, princes, statesmen in paragraphs on the historical background, as well as foreign composers (except for those connected with Hungary) are not enlisted.

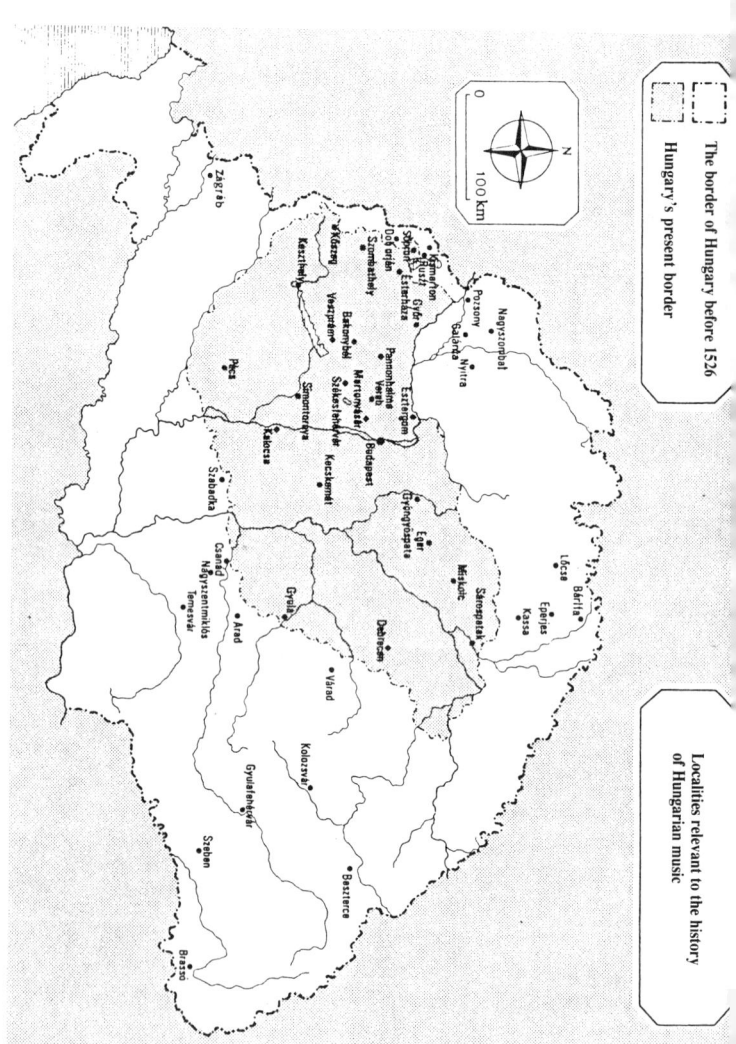

The border of Hungary before 1526

Hungary's present border

Localities relevant to the history
of Hungarian music

N

0   100 km

Zagráb

Kismarton
Sopron
Kőszeg
Szombathely
Dörögdön
Győr
Esterháza
Veszprém
Batanybói
Pannonhalma
Pécs
Várpalota
Esztergom
Márton vásár
Szabástvölke
Budapest
Simontornya
Kalocsa
Szabadka
Kecskemét
Nagyszombat
Pozsony
Galánta
Nyitra

Lőcse
Bártfa
Eperjes
Kassa

Eger
Gyöngyöspata
Sárospatak
Miskolc

Csanád
Nagyszentmiklós
Temesvár
Arad
Gyula
Debrecen

Várad
Kolozsvár
Gyulafehérvár
Szeben
Beszterce
Brassó